AF504736

Transnational Lives in China

Transnational Lives in China

Expatriates in a Globalizing City

Angela Lehmann
Xiamen University

palgrave
macmillan

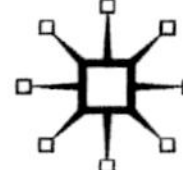

© Angela Lehmann 2014

All rights reserved. No reproduction, copy or transmission of this publication may be made without written permission.

No portion of this publication may be reproduced, copied or transmitted save with written permission or in accordance with the provisions of the Copyright, Designs and Patents Act 1988, or under the terms of any licence permitting limited copying issued by the Copyright Licensing Agency, Saffron House, 6–10 Kirby Street, London EC1N 8TS.

Any person who does any unauthorized act in relation to this publication may be liable to criminal prosecution and civil claims for damages.

The author has asserted her right to be identified as the author of this work in accordance with the Copyright, Designs and Patents Act 1988.

First published 2014 by
PALGRAVE MACMILLAN

Palgrave Macmillan in the UK is an imprint of Macmillan Publishers Limited, registered in England, company number 785998, of Houndmills, Basingstoke, Hampshire RG21 6XS.

Palgrave Macmillan in the US is a division of St Martin's Press LLC, 175 Fifth Avenue, New York, NY 10010.

Palgrave Macmillan is the global academic imprint of the above companies and has companies and representatives throughout the world.

Palgrave® and Macmillan® are registered trademarks in the United States, the United Kingdom, Europe and other countries.

ISBN 978–0–230–34839–4

This book is printed on paper suitable for recycling and made from fully managed and sustained forest sources. Logging, pulping and manufacturing processes are expected to conform to the environmental regulations of the country of origin.

A catalogue record for this book is available from the British Library.

A catalog record for this book is available from the Library of Congress.

Dedicated to the memory of
Felicity Lehmann
Anthropologist, writer and traveller
1948–2011

Contents

Acknowledgements

This research was made possible by the College of Arts and Social Sciences (CASS), Australian National University, Australia. A huge debt of gratitude is extended particularly to Dr Alastair Greig at CASS. His numerous readings and re-readings and the generosity of time spent with drafts of this work is the only reason this research has seen the light of day.

Peter and Jane Lehmann were a constant sounding board for my ideas and have put up with my endless questioning about their own times in China. Without them, this research would have been a much more arduous process. I am incredibly fortunate to have had the support and patience of my father during the research and writing process.

Many thanks to the people of Xiamen. To those who were interviewed for this research and those who put up with having a sociologist in their midst – especially while they were trying to have a good time – thank you. I am grateful to everyone in Xiamen who helped and supported me with this project. I would especially like to thank Li Weilin for her help and friendship.

Thanks also to the anonymous reviewers of this manuscript whose helpful comments have doubtless improved this work. Of course, all errors and faults lie solely with me.

Finally, thank you to Wayne Jones with whom I first 'met' Xiamen and who, throughout it all, remains my best friend, my muse and my happiness.

1
Introduction

The great escape

Research on migration from the West has expanded rapidly in recent years. The emergence of a burgeoning research discipline reflects an increased number of people from developed countries living and working between national boundaries and the anticipated effect this may have on both sending and receiving nations. It also reflects an increased interest in the social sciences in the everyday lives of those of a 'middling' level of transnational experience (Smith 2001). In other words, those who fit neither in the upper echelons of the transnational elite moving between highly paid jobs in major international centres nor in the unskilled or forced migrant group that represents the underprivileged and often disempowered face of globalization.

This growing group of migrants are middle class, relatively privileged and relatively well-educated people and have, until recently, been somewhat ignored from a grassroots, ethnographic perspective (Beaverstock 2002; Willis and Yeoh 2002). It is these transnational workers who will have an increasing impact on the way the world is shaped and the way that perceptions of cultural and social difference are interpreted and recreated on a daily basis. It is possible, indeed likely, that the middle classes from Europe, Australia and North America will have more and more experience as transnational workers living within Asia, particularly within China. Further, it is likely that rather than the traditional financial hubs of Shanghai and Hong Kong, emerging cities may attract increasing numbers of such migrants as new destinations within rapidly growing economies come to challenge traditional destinations (Skeldon 2010: 12).

Even after the global economic crises instigated by the 2008 banking collapse, China's economy seems to remain on the road to success, and in 2010 it overtook rival Japan to become the second biggest economy in the world. In a 2012 Pew Research Center Poll conducted in 21 countries, only an overall median of 27% thought their country's economy was doing well. In China, this figure was 83% (Pew Research Center 2013). China's development is surging forward and its people are overwhelmingly confident in their nation's increasing power on the world stage (Nye 2010). This confidence brings with it increasing assertiveness on the world stage and a turning of global attention towards China and the other emerging economies.

Meanwhile, reports from the West of increasing unemployment and harsh austerity measures continue. Unemployment has soared among youth across developed nations and those graduating into a recession can face long-term setbacks in their employment opportunities (Papademetriou, Sumption and Terrazas 2010). Graduates, with perceived fewer prospects in their home labour markets, are increasingly seeing the benefit of finding work in emergent markets. While still early in this process of 're-drawing the world in lots of ways and at lots of levels' (Aalbers 2009: 40), it is foreseeable that the numbers of young, professional migrants to Asian countries could increase. It is probable that in this current climate more people from the West will choose to leave home for career opportunities and work experience in Asia. The middle classes are more likely than ever before to pack up and leave their homes in the 'West' for the lands of supposed opportunity in the 'East'.

This phenomenon has been dubbed in the British media the 'Great Escape' as 'old-world escapees desperately seek exit strategies from economies in free fall' (Khaleeli, Smith and Smith 2013) and has led to murmurings of concern in Britain, the United States and Australia about a possible brain drain as professionals leave in search of a better life overseas (for example, see Murray et al. 2012; Ross 2012). The typical expat is now more likely to live in an emerging country than traditional European locations where they foresee that they can earn more and have a better lifestyle (Hydrogen Report 2012). While the most popular places to live abroad and work remain the United States, the United Kingdom and Australia, their dominance is waning and the emergent economies – in particular, the BRIC (Brazil, Russia, India and China) countries – are now seen as 'expat hotspots'.

This book explores the motivations, experiences and personal consequences of those who move between the developed 'West' and one city in mainland China. This research was conducted at a time of immense and rapid change in China and in an emerging city in order to better understand the way everyday lives are connected to wider notions of globality for this important and growing migratory type.

The gold rush

The Chinese city that forms the backdrop to the stories that follow is not a large, cosmopolitan city such as Shanghai or Guangzhou. Such cities are often discussed in sociological literature as 'global cities' (for example, Beaverstock 2002; Sassen 2001) which cater for mass movements of people from across the globe and function as a 'hub' for global financial flows. Shanghai, Guangzhou and, to a lesser extent, Beijing have a long established presence of foreign traders and business people and the city environment itself is often relatively easily navigated by non-Chinese, with established expatriate communities, groups and associations.

Instead, Xiamen, a second-tier city and an island in Fujian province, allowed for a contained community study. Xiamen was, and continues to be, an example of what Yeoh (2004) refers to as a 'globalizing city', indicating that world city-ness should be conceptualized according to different degrees of engagement with globality. At the time of this research, Xiamen could be seen as less 'global' than it is today.

By choosing to locate this study in a smaller, less 'global' city, I observed the various ways in which Western transnational workers negotiate cultural differences in what is perceived as a culturally distanced and sometimes 'illegible' environment. This allowed for an emphasis on the negotiation of notions of 'place' and how these impacted on the construction of identity and forms of community.

Xiamen is a coastal sub-provincial city in south-eastern Fujian province with a registered household population of 2.3 million at the time of research (Xiamen Municipal Government 2006). It became one of the first five Special Economic Zones in China in 1984, which means that the government encourages foreign direct investment and provides assistance and support for transnational corporations choosing to base their operations in the city. Xiamen (known to the West as 'Amoy' during the colonial era) has a history of foreign presence within the city, being one of the original treaty port cities following the Opium Wars between Britain and China in the nineteenth century (for discussion about Xiamen during this time, see Mackenzie-Grieve 1952 and Wood 1998). The foreign presence left after 1949, although since the 1980s it has been returning in a 'global' rather than 'colonial' guise.

Within eyeshot of Taiwan, Xiamen is a relatively wealthy city with money and goods flowing across the Straits. Xiamen is a major city in the home province of many of the world's Chinese diaspora and has benefited from their contribution to its economy and development. Xiamen port continues to increase in volume and capacity and since 1981 has remained one of the world's top 100 ports (China Briefing 2010).

Xiamen in 2013 is a very different experience to what it was seven years earlier. In this land where economic development is happening at a relative lightening pace, urban landscapes can completely change within weeks, let alone years. Xiamen is now home to China's largest Starbucks. Bars offer cocktails and live music along the water's edge and the expansive shopping malls could be like those in Singapore, London or Shanghai. The Porsche shop is located near the Lamborghini shop which is not far from the Ferrari dealership. The expatriate scene is nowadays well organized and diverse. Rugby and cricket tournaments are held frequently and the expat-favourite 'Hash Runs' are held regularly. Arriving at the heavily promoted beach parties is like walking into a beach party on a Thai island – hundreds, if not thousands of people from all over the world, dance the evening away under the stars.

This is the new China. This is an emerging international city with all the hallmarks of wealth and success and hyper-modernity. Yet this is not Shanghai or Hong Kong. Instead, this is a second-tier Chinese city, one of several such cities along the increasingly wealthy and industrialized eastern coastline.

In 2005, when the research presented in this book was conducted, Xiamen was on the cusp of becoming this ultra-modern city. At this time, the numbers of foreign investors arriving in the city were increasing, but there were still relatively few, what could be termed, 'Western facilities' there. It was still a city that was less well known to the West and yet the media and the locals would talk about how it was destined to become a 'mini Singapore'. The city and its planners and its people – both Chinese and foreign – were looking towards a global future for the city. The time that this research was conducted was a crucial point of change within the urban environment. Like the people I was studying, the city was reaching out to locate itself within the global economy.

This research, like other community studies, is confined in time and space, yet it does address questions of a wider global scale. This study is pertinent because it was conducted during a time of immense and rapid change for both China and Xiamen. It is an analysis of a transformative process of identity and solidarity for a group of people whose numbers are likely to increase in the current context. Xiamen cannot be seen as representative of all communities of transnational workers, yet the processes of change that are underway are transformations taking place in other cities across China and the world, making Xiamen an ideal 'laboratory' (see Stein 1960) for exploring the effects and meanings of these changes.

The stories that were told within this growing group of transnational workers spoke of a sense of being on the frontier of globalism. China, for them, was a land of economic promise and a land of the future. It was a time of 'gold rush fever'. China promised endless opportunities and the realization of ideas and emerging markets.

Yet those arriving from the West had no collective noun that they wore comfortably. The terms 'Westerner', *laowai* (foreigner), 'foreigner' and 'expatriate' were used interchangeably by members of this group and with a degree of unease. The problematic use of terminology is indicative of the central issues of identity and community in a transnational context. Throughout this book I refer to people I interviewed and interacted within Xiamen as alternatively Xiameners, Westerners, middling migrants, privileged migrants, skilled transnational workers and *laowai* – a common Mandarin term for foreigners. I use the term 'expatriate' in situations where the interviewees themselves would define themselves as such – often in contrast to other Westerners in Xiamen – a division which will be discussed in later chapters. This lack of a comfortable collective noun indicates a need for exploration and definition of such transnational communities and hints towards new senses of belonging and social division within a changing global context.

Transnational capitalists, lifestyle migrants or expatriates?

While it could be said that the study of middle-class migration from the 'West' to the 'East' is beginning to constitute a new field of migration research, there exists an uneasiness about where such migrants 'fit' within the literature. According to Fechter and Walsh (2010) there is an 'urgent need to develop nuanced understandings of these more privileged tiers of movement and to problematize them' (p. 19). The difficulty in finding a suitable collective noun for this group indicates a need to further explore how such forms of migration can be understood as both a continuance of historical processes and a new form of mobility. This migratory type should be conceptualized as a migration pattern that is characterized by choice and affluence, and as defined by boundaries and relative limitations. Research into Westerners living in Asia tends to classify or label these migrants as transnational elites, lifestyle migrants or postcolonial expatriates – each emphasizing different aspects of the relative power and freedom they have in making their decision to initially leave home in the developed 'West'.

The transnational capitalist class (Sklair 2001) or transnational elites (Beaverstock 2002, 2011) are highly skilled international migrants – transnational corporation executives or finance professionals, for example – and tend to be concentrated in global cities such as Singapore, Shanghai and Hong Kong. These elite migrants are major actors that create financial capital and tend to move on a corporate posting or in response to economic or corporate demand. Indeed, the middling migrants presented here do make their decisions in response to economic rationalities, and to an extent we can see that the flow of people does indeed follow the flow of money and corporate interest.

However, research has tended to focus on 'either end of the labour market, neglecting the middle' (Clarke 2005: 307, see also Farrer 2010). Those who participated in this study are more likely to follow Amit's (2007) claim that 'their more modestly prosperous situations likely reflect a much broader reorientation of global long-distance travel and movement around middle-class, rather than very affluent or very poor voyagers' (p. 3). Moreover, as we shall see, this group contains 'perhaps as many refugees from global capitalism as elite talents' (Farrer 2010: 1225). While the emerging markets do pull these migrants in terms of potential jobs and economic opportunities, this does not adequately reflect the complexities and nuances of individual narratives of leaving home (Castles 2010).

These decisions, whether elite or middle class, are made within specific social, cultural and historical contexts. According to Willis and Yeoh (2005), 'mobile sensibilities are shaped not just in response to corporate logic or economic rationalities alone but also in the context of social-cultural-political considerations operative at family-community-country scales' (cited in Yeoh and Huang 2011: 683). Research into lifestyle migration emphasizes the presentation of migration as a route to a better and more fulfilling way of life, especially in contrast to the one left behind (Benson and O'Reilly 2009a: 1). The search for the 'good life' manifests in the decision – whether this is explicit or not – to leave home in the West for a better way of life. As we shall see, the quest for leisure and escape is a central theme in the lives of those from the West living in China, and to a degree the participants of this research do fit in this category of lifestyle migrants – albeit often unwittingly.

It is imperative that the 'newness' of lifestyle migration and both elite and middle-class migration from the West be tempered with an awareness of the significance of the past in shaping Western mobilities. Indeed, the term 'expatriate' is awkward in terms of these newly emerging migratory experiences. 'Expatriate' carries historical baggage and indicates a type of migration from the West which is declining in prominence, that is, being employed at home and posted on an assignment, usually with a start and end date. From a researcher's perspective, the term carries with it a presupposition of national identity and allegiance, indicating a methodological nationalism and doing little to allow for the exploration of fluidities and multiplicities of national and ethnic identities.

The post-colonial is inherent within the shaping of contemporary expatriate mobilities and is essential to understanding constructions of identities and power relations that are both gendered and racialized within globalizing places. Fechter and Walsh (2010) suggest that contemporary expatriates or Westerners who live and work outside 'the West' may be regarded as the modern-day equivalents of European colonials and settlers. Yet, despite a recent surge of interest in such migrants (for example, Coles and Walsh 2010; Farrer 2010; Fechter 2007; Leggett 2005; Leonard 2008, 2010), studies into this group of people remain relatively scarce. This book explores how racial and power inequalities exist and are reconfigured and challenged (Fechter and Walsh 2010: 1198) on a daily basis by those from the West living in China.

The term 'middling migrant' is perhaps the best fit at present as a functional umbrella concept for each of these migratory types. The middling migrant is disconnected neither from the past as an expatriate in post-colonial Asia, nor from the future as a lifestyle migrant or a potential transnational elite. The middling migrant is situated locally and interacts with particular people on a daily basis.

Walsh (2007, 2012) talks about 'grounding' research on expatriate belonging. In other words, research should recognize that transnational belonging is constituted through everyday practices that are about both attachment and detachment. Such an approach to Western migratory experience emphasizes 'banal geographies' (Beaverstock 2011) and a useful starting point to uncovering the 'multiple subjectivities and differentiated power geometries' operating in transnational lives (Yeoh and Huang 2011: 688). Conradson and Latham's (2005a: 228) claim that the 'taken-for-granted texture of daily existence' can provide useful insights into the lived experiences of globalism for groups of migrants that have thus far been little examined. They argue:

> Viewed from this quotidian angle, even the most hyper-mobile transnational elites are ordinary: they eat; they sleep; they have families who must be raised, educated and taught a set of values.
>
> (Conradson and Latham 2005a: 228)

By focusing on these 'everyday' experiences of mobility and by studying one community of Western workers, I examine how gender, ethnicity and status define the creation of global citizens and the construction of localized contexts as these people devise ways to 'make themselves at home in the world' (Albrow et al. 1994).

The approach

In recent years China has often been represented as a kind of national manifestation of macro-economic processes of contemporary globalization. China is becoming a representation of the vulnerability associated with globalization and symbolic of the future of globality.

The rise of China as potentially the world's largest economy is reported daily in the media around the world. Major global issues which are the focus of contemporary debates concerning the side effects or consequences of globalization are frequently cited in relation to the rise of China's economy. Notions of the 'global' are constructed in popular and political discourses concerning human rights, international security, disease and public health, the environment, disaster management, free-trade and foreign investment and the staging of global events such as the Beijing Olympic Games. Each of these discourses on globalization are cited in the mass media as represented by China's national policy, its history, its rapid development, its approach to human rights issues, freedom of information, freedom of speech and responses to natural disasters. The future of globalization is often depicted as resting on the shoulders of China's success or failure.

A notion of China as 'representative' of these global processes was sought throughout interview data, particularly in terms of the reasons why people decided to leave for China initially. China, in this sense, was used in the measurement of transnationals' level of engagement with global integration and structural global change.

China was a setting that allowed for perceived cultural difference. In order to emphasize the experience of cultural difference, a city was chosen where an expatriate community was not yet established, yet was growing. I selected a city that could be seen as representative of the rapid changes taking place in China while still allowing for a site of assumed cultural difference which would need to be negotiated by transnational workers.

Interviews and observation

Thirty-five interviews were conducted with Americans, Europeans, Canadians, Australians, New Zealanders and one Singaporean, living either permanently or semi-permanently in Xiamen between May and November 2005. Interviewees came from a range of nationalities, age groups, lengths of stay and occupations in China.

The largest groups of interviewees were teachers (30%) and trade entrepreneurs (29%). Teachers were employed on a full-time basis with private language schools, state-run schools or universities or were working on a freelance basis with private students. Trade entrepreneurs were associated with small enterprises involved in developing products for export to North America, Australia and Europe. These trade entrepreneurs were either employed by small- to medium-sized businesses in their homeland or ran start-up companies, often involving one or two individuals living in Xiamen.

Those involved with marketing, charity work, hospitality or consulting made up 17% of respondents and what are known as 'trailing spouses', or partners of people who work in any of these roles but who do not work themselves, made up 14% of the respondents. Lastly, traditional 'expats' on large corporate packages with a contractual stay in China with multinational companies who employed them at home constituted 9% of the interviewees. This significantly smaller sample reflects a global trend towards employing better-educated, local middle management for lower salaries and conditions (Selmer 2004). Language students were not approached for interviews because it was felt that their limited stay in China, and their university support system, puts them in unique relationship to the city. However, students do make up a growing proportion of Westerners in Xiamen as universities market themselves to the West as a site for language tuition and establish relationships with universities abroad.

The nationality of respondents was split between Britain (25%), the United States (26%) and Australia (25%), while Canadians and continental Europeans (French, Dutch, Danish) each made up 9% and New Zealanders, 6%. Interviewees were from a range of ages, with fewer interviewed in the oldest age group, 51–60 years (14%), and the youngest two were under 21 years (6%). This appears to be consistent with the age demographics of skilled transnational communities globally, with most Western transnationals falling in the 31–40 and 41–50 age groups (Hugo, Rudd and Harris 2003; OECD 2002).

Interviewees were also distinguished according to the length of stay in Xiamen in order to note differences between new arrivals (less than 18 months, 26%), mid-term (less than three years, 40%) and long-term stayers (more than three years, 34%). This breakdown reflects a common perception among the community that was expressed to me on several occasions in Xiamen – that 'people either stay three months, three years or forever' (Field Diary 18 August 2005). These temporal markers provide a useful tool for mapping the way transience is perceived by those experiencing it.

Along with interviews, I conducted participant observation and was very much a part of the subject I was studying. The reflexive nature of this research was reflected in a field-journal and extensive notes.

The questions, theories and arguments that follow are thus worthy of further research and discussion in other contexts, particularly given current shifts in the global economic landscape and the possible effects these shifts may have on middling migration to developing nations. The rise of the economies of Asia, and China more specifically, is a part of the way that globalization is understood and experienced by those who participated in this research. However, this is not an Asian studies book. This is not a book about China. This is a book about the idea of 'The West' and what this means at the everyday level for those living in a very different environment to their homes. This is, primarily, a book about social theory and the impact of transnational migration from Western nations on contemporary sociology and the stories that we tell ourselves and each other about globalization.

The journeys

Rather than a phenomenon to be understood as an independent field of inquiry, migration should be seen as contextualized within larger, ongoing social relationships and processes of change. Migration – whether skilled or unskilled, privileged or unprivileged – is not a decontextualized reaction to economic forces and social events. Instead, the experience of mobility plays an integral role in creative processes and pushes forward newness into the world. Migration is both a reaction to and a creator of social change. As such, sociological ideas about identity, class, ethnicity, gender and status should be integrated with ideas about the ways that movement between borders and boundaries impacts on and shapes lives.

Castles (2010) argues for this need to embed migration research in a more general understanding of contemporary society. Migration, for Castles, needs to be seen as a normal part of social relations and theories of migration should help us to analyse the dynamics of migration, not in isolation, but as part of complex and varied processes of societal change (Castles 2010: 1568). This book follows this call to embed migration research and links migration narratives with broader social theory and societal change in general. Ethnographic data collected in Xiamen is used to engage in dialogue between everyday experiences of transnationalism and theories of global change.

I conceptualize this dialogue according to four theoretical journeys. First, I follow the territorial journeys of those living outside their homes in the West. The experience of being an outsider allows for the re-conceptualization of 'place'. The nation, the city, the suburb and the local environment contribute to and allow for the re-examination of boundaries of identity which were perhaps not visible in other, more familiar, places. My aim is to seek the relationship between mobility and stasis, or, as Smith (2001: 237) posits, to 'capture a sense of the distanciated yet situated possibilities for constituting and reconstituting social relations'. The focus here on place and territoriality leads this research to support what Ang (2000: 6) claims is the 'reconfiguration' of spatial distance and proximity, rather than their eradication in global contexts.

Second, the stories that follow recount structural journeys. Forms of power and restriction at home such as status, gender, race and nationality are likewise transformed as the territorial journey and the re-conceptualization of place allows for a time of questioning of the 'common-sense' social rules and norms of home. This time of questioning is a period of 'liminality', which allows for the later reconfiguration of social structure as a local community develops.

Third, this book is the story of emotional journeys. Much sociological literature describes how globalization can be seen as enhancing feelings of vulnerability and ambivalence as changes take place to the way we experience both place and structure. I explore postmodern claims that increasing mobility results in a condition of 'rootlessness' characterized by 'thin' forms of solidarity and a lack of emotional commitment both to others and to places (for example, Beck 2000; Hannerz

1996; Turner 1994, 2000; Turner and Rojek 2001). These claims of free-floating and rootless cosmopolitanism are explored by focusing on what I term vulnerable 'emotional structures'. Using this concept of emotional structures, I examine the way that emotional action is performed within structured and historicized boundaries of meaning. Three forms of vulnerable emotional structures are analysed here – anxiety, ecstasy and fear – in order to explore links between subjectivity and structure and between local experience and global mobility.

Recent years have seen an increase in interest in the social role of emotion in the lives of migrants (for example, Conradson and Latham 2005a; Svaek 2010; Walsh 2012). Walsh (2012) says this is due to a wider recognition in the social sciences of a need to ground migration research in the everyday, embodied lives of middle-class transnationals (Conradson and Latham 2005a). A focus on emotional geographies and a notion that 'emotions matter' are a part of this recognition as emotional geographies are intrinsically relational yet are not necessarily *in* the social nor the individual (Ahmed 2004: 10; Walsh 2012). The concept of the 'emotional structure' at once grounds research in the exploration of contextualized, embodied subjectivities and connects migrant lives to social structures, forms of power and the values that underpin globality.

Fourth, throughout the narratives that follow is an over-riding *moral* journey. Morality, in this sense, refers to the way that people position themselves and others with regard to wider value structures. I use the term 'moral landscape' to examine key values associated with being 'Western' and 'Global' (such as individualism, freedom and difference) and their relationship to the everyday experience of globalization (Figure 1). I conceptualize this value orientation as 'globalism' and consider this as being one of the multiple processes involved with what is known as 'globalization' (Albrow and King 1990). I adopt Albrow and King's (1990) and Steger's (2002) perspective that 'globalism' refers to a 'set of values' or 'value orientations' which underpin globalization (Albrow and King 1990). I have selected one such 'set of values' – individualism, freedom and difference – in order to understand the relationship between the experiences of global mobility and the values underpinning globalism. There are, of course, other such values which could be seen as underpinning globalism, such as rationality, progress and secularism (Steger 2002). The three values I analyse emerged within the data itself.

The journeys recounted here are transformative. They map a process of the loosening of structures in order to allow for their later

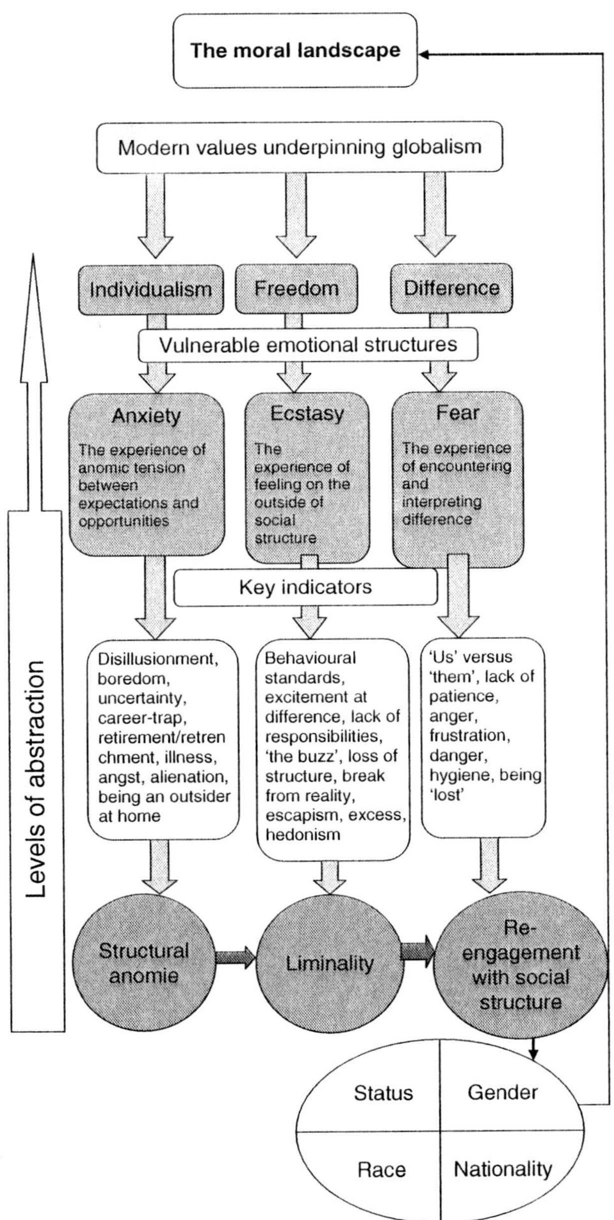

Figure 1 The moral landscape

reconstruction. It is at the everyday level of experience and place that being a *laowai*, an outsider, provides the essential context for this process to occur. While these journeys are specific to a time and place, they are a part of a larger narrative of global migration and the complex relationships between value structures, globalism and increasing mobility.

Part I
Vulnerabilities of Global Mobility

2
Anxiety and Individualism

The journey this book undertakes begins with the initial decision to leave home. The motivations that people in Xiamen expressed for leaving their homeland can be understood in terms of the demands of a global flexible workplace and in terms of changed understandings of time and place within a global, national and personal context. The value of individualism plays a central role in this decision to leave home and essentially 'become global'. The tension between value discourses of this heightened individualism and the contrasting expectations of the community results in a form of vulnerability – expressed here as the emotional structure of anxiety. Through exploring the connections between the values that underpin global mobility (such as individualism) and locally experienced emotional structures (such as anxiety) the transnational skilled worker can be viewed as simultaneously reacting against and contributing to globalizing processes.

The changing nature of place in the construction of identity can be seen by looking at the way time is constructed. Place and time are connected concepts and closely related to the value of individualism. Individualism is linked to the valuing of time as short term. According to some postmodern theory, the flexible, global workplace means that life-paths become increasingly fragmented. Long-term careers and stability are frequently cited as an experience and value of a past modern era (Rifkin 2000; Sennett 2006). Understanding the way that places are perceived as temporal constructions is vital to uncovering the meanings that territoriality holds for those living global lives.

An ethnography of transnationalism can be seen as an ethnography of movement both between places and throughout time. Time and place are hence reconstructed together as people make decisions about their life-course – where they will go, where they have come from and where they are now. It became clear through Xiameners' responses to questions about life narratives that home was an important 'territorial' concept bound with moral and temporal implications.

For people who choose to leave the territoriality of their origin, 'home' becomes a place in the past and a place in the perhaps distant future. The idea of home is a temporally situated place which is produced in relation to the landscape of 'now'. The meanings attached to place are seen here to be located in other places and at other times. This perspective supports Jameson's (1988: 121) assertion that 'the truth of experience no longer coincides with the place in which it takes place'. Likewise, the truth of experience no longer necessarily coincides with the time in which it takes place. This signifies the continuing relevance of place, yet demonstrates a need for re-conceptualization of concepts of territoriality, locality and the role of 'home'.

Narratives of motivations to leave the place in the past called 'home' reveal much about relationships to the present place and the way that identity and belonging are reconstructed within it. Furthermore, these narratives of life-paths are inevitably moral; that is, they point to a positioning within larger frameworks of time and place. This 'positioning of self' occurs alongside the construction of meanings attached to place (whether 'home' or 'away') and is a concept I refer to as the 'moral landscape' (Figure 1).

The reasons why Western transnational workers in Xiamen decided to leave home and the processes that led to this decision unveiled a sense of anxiety and disillusionment with home. Rather than coming 'to' China, it seemed that most people I spoke to were 'going away from' their home. The source of this anxiety is neither singular nor generalizable. Each person I encountered or interviewed in Xiamen had their own 'unique' tale to tell about their journey leading up to their arrival in China. Each felt that their story was exceptional – that they, somehow, were different from people at home and other foreigners they had met in Xiamen. These stories of leaving home were stories of the value of individualism.

It was the experience of facets of this individualism (such as individual choice, freedom and flexibility) that was to form the initial decision to leave home, and eventually to form the basis of the reconstitution of communities in Xiamen. The sources of this individual anxiety were at 'home' and Xiamen was hence conceptualized as a place, and a time that, in various ways, was perceived in relation to these notions of individualism and anxiety.

While each story was seen as unique by the teller, there were commonalities or themes which arose among the accounts of motivations to leave home. These major themes concern a common narrative of fragility and anomie. The first theme concerns accounts of anxiety and disillusionments with home. A common feeling of precariousness or instability in terms of the workplace, career, relationships, community and meaning was spoken about by many Western people in Xiamen. The second theme addresses accounts of relationships to time and place in terms of motivations to leave home.

The examples I draw with relation to both these themes are interrelated. The first theme explores the reasons people gave for leaving their homeland, and the second theme explores the way narrative was structured in terms of locating the self within a life-path and within a local and global context.

Precarious lives: The tensions of individualism

The dilemma of the flexible workplace

One effect of the rise of neo-liberal global capitalism has been the concurrent rise of what Beck (1999) terms the value of individualism – that is, the widely shared patterned belief that we make our way in the labour market on our own initiative. Beck (1999, 2000) argues that in this context we, as individuals, are increasingly considered responsible for the course of our career and our social life. The centrality of the individual in terms of agency and accountability in the global era is a social value insofar as it is a system of beliefs that is produced, performed and resisted within social structure and within empowered interactions.

For some theorists, it is this distinct shift towards an overwhelming perception of individual choice and accountability that differentiates the present era of globalization from the previous era. Sennett (1998, 2006) has pointed to the disorienting effects of globalization on personal life – particularly on how today's world of impermanent contract work sets the inner life adrift. Likewise, Beck (2000: 19) suggests that we are currently moving towards a 'second, open, risk-filled modernity characterized by general insecurity'. This 'second' modernity has been described by Beck (2000) as 'reflexive', in the sense that it increasingly has to face the unintended and unwanted consequences of its own success. As Beck (2000: 21) states:

> To express this in a metaphor, we are dealing here with a 'revolution of side-effects'. Concepts such as 'ambivalence', 'unclarity', but also others such as 'disorientation' seem to become more not less significant as these changes take effect.

Such side effects, suggests Beck, are the unintended consequences of the individualism which has accompanied the move into an era of globalism. Sociology, and privileged migration studies in particular, needs to take into account not only the personal consequences of globalization but also the global consequences of 'personalization' or individualism. This chapter explores this idea further by conceptualizing anxiety as the localized and personalized experience of tensions between the values of individualism and the community. The decision to leave home is made within this context of structural tension and demonstrates the continuing and linked relevance of place, structure and emotion for transnational sociality.

The Westerners I interviewed and spoke with in Xiamen spoke often at length about the reasons they came to China. These narratives situated the self within a context of larger global and national processes that they felt they were a part of (or, as we shall see, on the margins of). Narratives necessarily recount a story as a personal temporal sequence that occurs within these larger processes. Thus, stories of why people left home were important accounts of how time and place were perceived as a part of these global processes and the individual experience and production of them. For many, leaving home for Xiamen was a reaction against an anomic state of anxiety within this context of globalism.

Anxious careers: Simon and Sarah

Simon sits at a popular Western bar in Xiamen sipping his third Heineken. It's a Tuesday night and the speakers resound with music that was popular in his home country, the United Kingdom, more than 10 years ago. Simon has been in China for seven years and in Xiamen for five. He is comfortable on his bar stool. He knows the bar staff and puts his drinks on a 'tab' which is paid whenever he can.

Back in England, Simon has finished five years of university and in Xiamen he works for a trading company exporting small toys and giftware to the United States and the United Kingdom. He graduated with Honours and speaks some German, French and now conversational Mandarin. He describes his family as middle class – his mother is a teacher and his father runs a successful business. He is well spoken, intelligent and his friendliness is evident in the numerous people who stop past, buy him a drink and have a chat about golf, the football and the goings-on in town.

At 34 years old, Simon[1] appears to fit the mould of the highly educated and well-off young people who are being discussed across Western nations as leaving national boundaries and inducing a potential state of brain drain (Hugo, Rudd and Harris 2003; OECD 2002, 2003, 2004).

Simon's apparent openness to others, his active movement around the globe and his multi-lingual skills point towards a sense of cosmopolitanism or flexible transnationalism. At face-value, Simon is privileged and has actively chosen to leave home to reap the benefits of processes of economic globalization. Simon has the educational and financial resources to make the value of individualism beneficial to him. He can effectively choose to leave the United Kingdom, to travel, and can do so with economic resources behind him.

People like Simon are a vital part of the process of globalization that is so often spoken about in terms of the global push towards democratic, Western, neo-liberal economic and cultural ideologies (see Robinson 2004; Sklair 2001; Steger 2002). If the opposite of social control is choice, then Simon should represent a triumph for the modern ideal of the free individual. His choice to leave home appears an expression of individual freedom of choice.

However, the so-called context of 'freedom' within which these choices are made can be questioned. The motivations of Simon and other Western transnational workers to leave home are in fact a part of larger narratives of tension between values of individualism and of being a social 'outsider' which lead to a sense of anomie. The move to Xiamen can be seen as representative of the performance of the resultant emotional structure of anxiety.

Before coming to China, Simon was working for the civil service in a Northern English city. After graduating he found himself logging births, deaths and marriages in the Certification Division of his local government. He says:

> I guess I came here because of disillusionment. If you were to sum it up it would be disillusionment. A little bit with the job that I was in, the country that I was living in, the system that I was living within.
>
> But at the time I left it was basically just leaving England to do something for a year – that's what I thought at the time – that was a little bit different. When I was in England I thought I was pretty hot shit. It sounds pretty conceited to say that but I thought I wasn't punching my weight in England. I thought I was capable of doing a lot more and better things. Unfortunately, the way the job market was working in the United Kingdom at the time, there wasn't much room for a relatively fresh university graduate to do that much.

> For me, personally, getting around Manchester you find yourself in a precarious position. I have experience, or I had experience in many different places and areas as far as jobs go. I went to university, got the degree – albeit that it wasn't a particularly vocational degree [Cultural Studies], it was more or less an academic degree…So after leaving university the jobs that I wanted were difficult to get. The jobs that I could do quite easily, the employers would take one look at my CV and say sorry, you're not qualified for the job. For me, personally, it doesn't really matter what I do. I'll do anything as long as I'm earning money. But as soon as you've got a degree those jobs are automatically cut away from you because they know you're only going to be around as long as it takes you to get another job.
>
> So for the good jobs, the competition is too great, for the bad jobs you are unemployable. I didn't have the right experience in the job marketplace. So unless you're incredibly lucky or incredibly talented, it's difficult for you to get a job.
>
> I had no interest in China before coming here. I knew nothing about China. I didn't know a single person who had been to China. Apart from Mr Yip at the local fish and chip shop.

Simon's story of his decision to come to China, like many others in Xiamen, describes how profound changes underway in the post-industrial global world of work and the marketplace are negotiated and performed within local contexts. According to theorists such as Beck, Sennett and Bauman, increasingly flexible workplaces and the decline of traditional careers-for-life mean that we must now decide for ourselves, as individuals rather than members of a profession, a family, a community, how our working lives will unfold.

According to such theorists, each person is seen as responsible for their own future – not only in terms of what job to take next, but increasingly in terms of where to take this job. As a result, the options about where my life can take me can appear endless, yet should I fail, then the responsibility is mine alone. Self-discipline and self-fashioning came together in Weber's Protestant individual who had to shape his or her history so that it would add up to a meaningful, worthy whole (Weber [1905] 2001). Weber's theology of the individual today has profound resonance for those who can now actively use the globe to build their own 'do-it-yourself' biographies (Beck 2000; Rosenthal 2005).

However, this is an era characterized by the maxim 'my life, my failure' rather than any other worldly pre-destination (Rosenthal 2005).

The instability of the short-term flexible workplace means that global movement is itself both the cause and the effect of anxiety over the individualization of life-choices and the global setting for these choices to be made. One interviewee, a 59-year-old English teacher from Canada said: 'This is my life. Accept it. If you don't like it, wait 'til your contract's up and go somewhere else.'

From the perspective of Beck, Sennett and Bauman, the global workplace in this era is a setting for the production of this new individualism, as well as its side effects. Changes in the workplace such as increased outsourcing and contract-based, short-term employment mean that paid employment is becoming precarious and normal life-stories are breaking up into fragments as our lives no longer follow a traditional linear and territorial pattern:

> One future trend is clear. For a majority of people, even in the apparently prosperous middle layers, their basic existence and life-world will be marked by endemic insecurity.
>
> (Beck 2000: 3)

According to this perspective, our personal biographies are increasingly built according to market forces. We create and sell our experiences as 'individuals' in the marketplace. More and more people are encouraged to perform as a 'Me & Co.' – an individually packaged *curriculum vitae* which can be continually built, changed and adapted according to the demands of the market (Beck 2000: 2). This marketplace is now intricately global, however, and these global flows combined with this individualism and insecurity result in a 'Global Me & Co.' where the world is a setting for the construction of these individual biographies. Beck's claim that our lives are increasingly marked by insecurity and vulnerability was supported by the interviewees' stories. However, Beck's theory supposes that this insecurity is a passive and unintended personal consequence of an individualism tied to the rise of global neo-liberalism. The interviewees' tales, however, told of a more active decision-making process which was a means to palliate or reassert control over the structural anxiety felt at home.

This relationship between individualism and transnationalism from the West is supported by Conradson and Latham's (2005b) study of New Zealanders living in London. In interviews with ten relatively young, well-educated middling migrants (Smith 2001) living in London, Conradson and Latham (2005b: 290) found that while decisions to move appeared to be highly 'individualistic' they were 'in fact enfolded within a range of established and enduring social relationships' connected to other geographical locations, particularly 'home'. They noted that the decision to leave New Zealand for London was expressed in narratives of self-realization and development which, while supporting claims of hyper-individualized biographies, emerged from a particular historical and geographical culture of mobility (Conradson and Latham 2005b). Conradson and Latham (2005b: 299) conclude that this decision to leave home points to 'subtle and skilled negotiations of the emergent structures of globalisation'. One such negotiation is located in the tension between the value of individualism and the continued norms of the community at home.

Likewise, research into lifestyle migration has highlighted the emphasis in migration stories on individualized, self-realization narratives in the decision to migrate. For such lifestyle migrants the decision to leave home releases them from ties and allows them to live lives more 'true to themselves' (Benson and O'Reilly 2009). These decisions are made as part of their reflexive projects of the self, or, as Hoey (2005) describes it, as an escape from disillusionment through seeking an alternative lifestyle. Research into lifestyle migration and skilled transnational migration would benefit from questioning the distinctions between their subject groups. Blurred boundaries between leisure and work are increasingly leading to 'overlapping of categories of travel' (Amit 2007: 5) and simplifying motives into either one box or another is no longer always possible. Studies of privileged migration more generally should question the notion of 'choice' which frame people's decisions to leave by focussing on the tensions that may push people away from one place and towards another. Rather than merely a quest for money, or even an increased standard of living, the decision to leave home is also often a pull towards the creation of a 'unique' individual life-path and biography.

The stories described by the Xiameners suggest that, if our do-it-yourself biography doesn't include the individual means to achieve its socially desired ends, a viable alternative for many is to escape these social expectations and leave for a different place where individual means and ends can be again reconfigured. This adds agency to Beck's (2000) claims that the flexible global workplace results in uncontrollable insecurity and passive vulnerability. The decision to become global can be seen as not only a reaction to value tensions but also an action which attempts to assert resistance to the tensions between the value of individualism and the expectations of the community.

Simon was anxious about his inability to 'fit' into the job market in England. He felt he had diverse skills and education, yet was in a position of instability and angst about how his 'biography' could be created to take best advantage of who he felt he should be. Eventually, leaving England for China was a means of escaping the emotional structure of anxiety that is associated with global flexibility by leaving the structures of home for somewhere perceived as different and outside of the realm of choice at home.

A similar story of disillusionment with the flexible workplace was spoken about by Sarah who left Washington for China after the dot-com bubble burst in the early 2000s. Sarah had developed skills in a diverse range of industries back home. She had spent time as a pathologist, a hospital administrator, a teacher, within advertising and public relations and IT. She holds tertiary qualifications in hospital pathology and had at one stage begun a degree in English literature. Like Simon, she sees herself as flexible in terms of her skills, her education and in terms of what she is willing to do career-wise. But it was the diversity and flexibility of her skills that were to lead to the sense of non-fulfilment and disenchantment with her career and her eventual decision to leave the United States for China:

> I was looking for work after a job contract had ended. I sent out a hundred emails and letters and got two responses and one interview. It was just after the dot-com bubble had burst in Seattle which is where I'm from and it was a very bad time to be looking for work, I guess unless I wanted to work in a laboratory drawing blood which is what I did at university, I probably would not have found a job that had equal compensation.

> I went to a temp agency and they said 'oh, it looks like you'd make a very good hospital assistant' which means changing bed pans. And I thought, I don't need to go and be a hospital assistant. I spoke to my university hospital about opening a department for rewriting the research papers that were being published for the university press. There are a lot of people in the hospitals who were very good technically but they can't really write. They just said, maybe next year. It was too long to wait.

> I ran out of money and I had to make a decision. I wanted to go somewhere so far away from the society I was living in. At that point I wanted to go to the most foreign place. I wanted to go somewhere that was really foreign. The job in China offered that possibility.

Both Simon and Sarah described their decision to come to Xiamen as the result of a series of frustrations with the structure of the labour market at home. Their narratives spoke of a sense of profound individualism – a sense that their personal biographies were not unfolding according to social expectations. They considered themselves multi-skilled in a variety of industries, held higher educational qualifications and expressed a willingness to work. Both considered themselves ideal members of the contemporary flexible post-structural workplace with their accreditation and skill base. Yet neither could achieve the goals they set.

It could be argued that Simon, Sarah and others in Xiamen were experiencing a form of anomie (Durkheim [1898] 1973; Merton [1938] 1973). Leaving home for Xiamen was an expression of an anomie which was global in its causes and in its effects. It was the flexible, global workplace that resulted in the tensions between the value of individualism and the expectations of the community. Yet it was also in reaction to these same tensions that those in Xiamen made the decision to leave home and essentially become 'global' – a process which served to produce and further the very values that underpin the structural setting from which the original tension was drawn. Farrer's (2010) study of long-term Western settlers in Shanghai describes this group as containing 'perhaps as many "refugees" from global capitalism as elite talent' (p. 1225). To some degree this is true of some of the Xiameners such as Simon and Sarah who left home with a sense of frustration and anxiety. However, the decision move was more complicated than either escape or engagement with globality. Instead, the decision to leave home can be seen as an active attempt to reassert control over working lives and biographies.

According to theorists such as Beck (2000), Sennett (2006) and Rifkin (1995), Simon and Sarah should be in a position of advantage in the post-industrial flexible workplace which rewards and places value on attributes such as adaptability and versatility. In reality, these skills left them with a feeling of 'floating' (male, 43, UK) and not quite fitting into any particular career path or job. They felt a tension between being over-qualified and under-qualified, under-skilled and over-skilled. Both left home to escape what they perceived as the precarious or vulnerable position they were in, despite describing themselves as almost ideal flexible workers.

The decision to leave home for many respondents was not about China in particular. It was about China as a foreign place, a different place which would perhaps provide some solidity or stability to the increasingly uncertain lives they were living at home. This process is connected to constructions of 'Western' identities and is a performance of what it means to be from 'the West'. In Yeoh and Willis' (2005) study of Singaporean expatriates living in China, this sense of China being a 'different cultural experience' was absent from respondents' narratives about China. Instead, Singaporean transnationals in China reported encountering China as a cultural 'return-to-roots' experience and a reconnection with the 'motherland'. Time, for these migrants, was imagined differently to Western expatriates with 'aimless wandering discouraged in Singapore's goal oriented society' (Yeoh and Willis 2005: 274).

Singaporean expatriates' decisions to leave for China may have indeed been instigated by a tension or an anxiety between competing notions of heritage and 'Chinese-ness'. However, for the Western migrants in Xiamen the move was towards a place of perceived cultural difference as a means to palliate the emotional structure of anxiety. Notions of place, structure and emotion were relevant to the decision to 'become global' even from these early stages. The decision to leave home was often made in order to encounter a perceived alternative to the familiar moral landscape of home in the 'West'.

The dilemma of fringe-dwelling

The tension between the value of individualism and the expectations of community extends from the workplace into the realm of relationships, identity and meaning. What to consume and who to identify with at 'home' often led to a daunting proliferation of choice for those I spoke with in Xiamen. This abundance of choice has led to theorists discussing the notion of 'flexible citizenship' (Ong 1999) and also 'cosmopolitan fallibilism' (Appiah 2006) as decisions can always be changed or altered and an alternative found.

This choice of identity can lead to a sense of being an 'outsider' at home. For some, the result of being an 'outsider' is to leave home to search for the great promise of the preferred choice. This experience of being an 'outsider' is evidence for the continued relevance of social structure in globally mobile lives.

According to Blakewell (2010), studies of underprivileged and forced migrants deny ascribing any agency to such people in their decisions to leave home. Meanwhile, it can perhaps be also claimed that studies of privileged or middling migration can be charged with the opposite – denying the structural constraints and local and community contexts of migration decisions and the complex ways that notions of individuality and social structure are experienced in everyday Western lives.

Further, the choice to leave home does not render 'place' insignificant in the construction of identity. Rather, the processes described here involve a reconfiguration of the way places (both 'home' and 'away') are used and conceptualized and provide evidence of their continuing relevance in the life-paths and moral landscapes of those living between borders.

Narratives of 'not-fitting in' (female, 28, Australia) at home were not restricted to discussions about the workplace. Many people that I interacted with and interviewed in Xiamen would describe themselves as being 'on-the-outside' at home in terms of social relationships, family and local and national politics. If not specifically talking about themselves, other foreigners in Xiamen were often described in conversation as a person who would be considered 'weird', 'strange' or 'outsiders' at home.

This sense of being an outsider at home was centred on notions of not being able to, or wanting to, comply with the rules and structures of their home society. This experience of being on the 'outside' demonstrates the continued relevance of social structure and community expectations. The decision to leave home and 'become global' was a result of a tension experienced as the emotional structure of anxiety between the value of individualism and these community norms.

Anxious identities: Marion and David

Marion is an Australian entrepreneur who had been in China for nearly 10 years at the time of my interview with her. She arrived on a contract with a large multi-national corporation and, two years prior to my interview with her, she left the company to study Chinese language and start her own export business dealing with jewellery and fashion accessories.

> I think our [home] society keeps us nice, you know, keeps us acting nice – putting on our happy faces. But here you can just be aaagggghhhhhhh! [screams and waves hands in the air] And nobody cares! During the day of course, you probably keep to yourself, but you can be more to the extremes here. You can go from being really slow to being really out of control and then somewhere in between to get work done. Whereas in Australia or Europe or wherever you would be seen as being on the fringe of society. You know, you're a weird character.

The decision to leave home for China for some was driven by a feeling of being a social outsider within their homeland. At a bar, a restaurant or at the beach on the weekend, Westerners would frequently talk about how 'he/she' would be considered a 'nerd, a geek, a weirdo, a sleaze, unfashionable, daggy' if they were 'back home'. But here, in this foreign place, these labels and their signifiers no longer applied in the same way. Decisions to leave home were instigated in many cases by a feeling of being 'on the fringes' (female, 45, Australia) of society at home – in terms of identity, consumption and interests.

David was a 30-year-old trade entrepreneur from London. In his spare time he was an artist and paints with oils and water-colours, as well as reading and writing copiously. As a child, David said he was constantly relocating with his family around the United Kingdom. Yet his family didn't really understand his desire to travel. Relocations were made through necessity for his father's work rather than through priorities being placed on seeing and doing new things. This pattern of moving as a child meant David never really felt he 'belonged' anywhere, and his lack of desire for money and his passion for art meant that in London as a young adult he also felt an outsider:

> I've always been kind of selfish in a way. As long as I've got enough money to get by and eat and do the things I want to do then that's ok with me. I have no interest in buying property. I don't have that kind of money anyway, but if I did, I don't think I'd be that keen on doing it. I'm not interested in being super rich.

> It was nice to cut yourself off from that for a while for me – I really enjoyed that. I thought, I'm glad I've got nothing to do with that. I don't care if I've got an opinion on [local politics or happenings in London] or not. What I am doing is totally selfish and I'm enjoying that, you know, that isolated feeling.

The traveller is often regarded as an outsider at home, before the decision is made to leave. Indeed, travellers and sojourners have long been associated with people who feel this sense of being an 'outsider at home'. The character of the 'stranger' (Simmel [1900] 1978), the 'outsider' (Elias 1965; Merton [1938] 1973), the 'marginal man' (Park [1928] 1969), the 'poet' (Berman 1983; Steegmuller 1996) and the traveller (MacCannell [1979] 1999) appears throughout modern literature. This experience of being an 'outsider' remains a valid and important facet of the lived experience of global processes even in the age of increasing individualism where many theorists assert the demise of community, solidarity and tradition. The experience of the social 'outsider' is evidence of the continued relevance of the 'inside' – that is, of solid or thick forms of solidarities which produce norms, boundaries and expectations. Rather than rootless and ambivalent cosmopolitans, the context within which the decision was made to leave the place of home is characterized by thick forms of solidarity and the emotional structure of anxiety.

The decision to become more mobile indicated the very real and continued demands, norms and expectations of one place – home. This decision to leave was a performance of the emotional structure of anxiety, and was not a performance of de-structured, free-floating cosmopolitanism.

The paradoxical pulls between the responsibilities of heightened individualism while at the same time recounting a sense of being on the 'outside' of a social group, culture and community led many to make the decision to leave home. It is globalism itself that therefore becomes both the cause *and* the consequence of the relationship between increasing mobility and the value of individualism; that is, the moral landscape of globalism (which encompasses values such as individualism) is constructed within the localized context in which the decision to 'become global' is made. This decision to leave home results in the active furthering of the moral landscape of globalism. This relationship between local places and the values that underpin globalism indicates the ongoing centrality of notions of place, structure and emotion for the context of heightened mobility.

Elliott and Lemert (2006) describe this new individualism as characterized by a tension between the processes of globalization and the increased 'privatization of selves'. The highly individualized language of globalization is hence a double-edged phenomenon – one that promotes the realization of self-fulfilment as well as the cultivation of self-limitation (Elliot and Lemert 2006: 12). The profoundly personal dilemma faced by those who chose to leave their homes in the industrialized West for Xiamen is likewise a manifestation of the more abstract dilemma between the promotion of individualism and the boundaries of community expectations. In this context, concepts of time and place become reconstructed as a means to resolve the crisis between the individual and community in the global era.

Motivations to leave and the use of time and place

The decision to leave home for many in Xiamen was the result of the experience of a form of anomie in terms of the workplace and community, expressed in terms of the tension between individual identity and collective belonging. The pull between the value structure of individualism and contrasting notions of being a social outsider resulted in the choice to leave home. This anomie was hence global and local in both its causes and effects and thus holds implications in terms of the ways that people in Xiamen were constructing and imagining notions of time and place in their everyday lives.

This sense of anomie at home led to a reconsideration of the ways that concepts of time and place can be *used* in order to situate the decision to move within ongoing biographical narratives. Narratives of time and place for the people I spoke to in Xiamen indicated a nexus between the local experience and the value structures that underpin globalism. This situating of the self within the moral landscape (see Figure 1) at the point of leaving home becomes vital in understanding the changes and reconstructions of self and identity after arrival in Xiamen.

Three approaches to time and place are discussed here. Each example has in common the theme that time and place were being used or manipulated in order to negotiate the dilemma between the values of individualism and community at home.

The cult of short-termism

According to Beck (2000), the short-term, flexible post-industrial workplace leads to new values, aims and fears. In this context, time is increasingly fragmented as life-courses are broken into shorter segments which do not necessarily flow progressively within a traditional 'career' pattern (Beck 2000). Flexibility, adaptability and living for the 'next job on the horizon' become values for the post-industrial worker which are constructed in opposition to what are perceived as 'traditional' values such as the long-term commitment and stability. To be a successful worker in this setting, time must be constructed as more and more fragmented and short term.

Likewise, global consumption, multi-media, communication technology and flows of cultural products across political and geographical boundaries mean that, for postmodern theorists, place is no longer valued as fixed, stable and constant. From this perspective, places now 'come to us' and we 'to them' through email, the Internet, the film, television and music industries, affordable air travel and multi-national companies producing and selling across borders. These constructions of place as shifting-yet-connected exist hand in hand with constructions of time as short term and fragmented. The personal consequences of these constructions of place and time in the era of globalism are an increased value being placed on the short term. Places, in this context, are imagined as being for *now*, not forever. From the postmodern perspective, the so-called demise of place exists hand in hand with the construction of time as short term.

In fact the construction of time and place as short term, or transient, is performed within discourse in relation to what are perceived as negative opposites. The long-term, the stable and the progressive, linear career path were spoken about by many Xiameners using terms such as 'mundane' (male, 34, England), 'dull' (male, 28, New Zealand) and 'normal' (female, 31, Australia). This negative view of the long term, of time and place as constants, led many to decide to leave a home that was perceived as a location of the potentially mundane.

The place of the mundane: Matthew

I met Matthew in a coffee shop that was popular with a trendy set of middle-class young Chinese people. Using perfect Oxford English, he apologizes for speaking slowly and using bad grammar: 'I never speak English anymore', he smiles. Matthew arrived in China from England six years ago. He describes himself as a political economist and at the moment he is conducting research for a prestigious London-based university. When he arrived in China he taught English as a freelancer and has spent time in several cities around mainland China. Ten months ago he arrived in Xiamen.

Like many others I met and interviewed in Xiamen, Matthew fit the mould of the growing numbers of skilled Westerners leaving home. He is young (mid-30s), highly educated and describes himself as 'embarrassingly middle class'. Matthew, like many others, describes his decision to leave home for China in terms of anxiety about both time and place:

> I think I came to China because of some kind of fear of an organized and planned future. I was afraid of the predictability and lack of challenge that came with life in England. I think many people come here with similar experiences in this regard. I needed a challenge and I needed to realize my own limitations. Home was boring. I wasn't ready for a set pattern to my life and loved the wonderful chaos that China offered. I wanted to mess my life up. China is messy. It is chaotic. It is unpredictable. And it changes before your eyes. Buildings go up so quickly here, change is rapid and constant. At home things are so slow – doing anything takes time, process and bureaucracy. A building goes up in China at the same speed as it takes to clean a window at home.

> I love the buzz of China. The uncertainty and instability of it all.
> You always have the feeling here that all of this change, this progress
> could all collapse, it could all collapse at any time. As quickly as it
> goes up, it can come down.

This fear of mundanity, of the long term, is closely linked to the value of individualism which emphasizes choice and do-it-yourself biographies. According to Elliot and Lemert (2006), the anxiety of not making the right choice 'for me' is becoming the emotional backdrop of globalization and the cult of the short term arises as a means to develop and uphold the values of individualism.

Matthew wanted change, uncertainty, chaos – the short term and ephemeral. In England, he was anxious that life would become stable, secure and boring – the long term. Leaving for China allowed him to realize the value he placed on the short term. Emotion (here seen through the emotional structure of anxiety), values (here seen as individualism) and place (here seen as 'home' and Xiamen), rather than becoming irrelevant to lives and identity in the global era, are instead being reconfigured together and are part of the expression and resistance to continued global processes.

Matthew's depiction of home as the site of the 'mundane' and the 'long term' and 'stability' suggests that Beck's theory that the Western post-industrial workplace is the setting for the construction of short-term flexibility needs to be framed in a bigger picture. Models of 'rootless cosmopolitanism' are only a snapshot of larger processes. Such arguments need to consider the continued long-termness and thick sociality of 'home'.

Accumulating time and place

Others in Xiamen, like Matthew, used or constructed notions of time and place in a way that would allow them to build or create their individual life-stories in a manner that they felt would add value to their longer-term biographical *curriculum vitae* upon return home.

According to many postmodernists, in our 'do-it-yourself society', we are now all entrepreneurs of our own lives (Beck 2000; Rosenthal 2005). For such theorists, increasingly we are said to be feeling individually responsible for the construction of ourselves as experienced, flexible workers whose worth is measured on the short-term labour market. Ideas of cosmopolitanism and flexible transnationalism emphasize this short-term attachment to careers, ideas, others and places. For many in Xiamen, time and place were being accumulated as a valuable commodity that could be taken home in the future and sold for social or financial capital. Time spent *here now*, in this distanced and different place, will help me back *there* in the *future*. The value placed on the short term described by Beck (2000) is found within the Xiameners' narratives, but this value exists as a part of a much longer journey which involves a continued relevance of long-term stability and thick notions of solidarity.

Travel in its various forms is essentially a consumptive and relational practice (Robinson and Phipps 2003: 5). Williams and Hall (2002) label contemporary forms of privileged migration 'tourism-informed mobility'. In other words, the choice to move can be seen as a consumptive act which 'gives a material form to a particular narrative of self-identity' (Giddens 1991: 81; also Benson and O'Reilly 2009a, 2009b). This consumption and accumulation have two related aspects for the individual in Xiamen. The first is the consumption of China as place and as 'global life experience'. Experience in Xiamen was paid for with a currency measured as time. Many Xiameners spoke of 'doing time' (male, 38, US) or 'spending time' (female, 20, UK) *here*, in order to increase social or economic status back home.

The second aspect of this consumption of place is this perceived added value of the commodity of China-experience once the person returned home to the West. This time–place product was then to be 'sold' in terms of higher social status or wider job choice for a greater value upon return. Conradson and Latham's (2005b: 292) study of Antipodeans living in London found similar results that describe the time spent abroad as 'the anxious and energetic assembling of experience as part of a naked attempt to assemble cultural capital to be deployed when one returns home'. Time in China was seen as a particularly valuable personal asset with regard to the discourse of China as the new land of promise 'where change is happening right now' (female, 26, Australia). Participants in Farrer's (2010) study of long-term Western settlers in Shanghai also recounted 'being in the right place at the right time' and 'catching the waves' of commerce which Farrer describes as narratives of emplacement which focus on 'nostalgia for the future' (p. 1221).

China is frequently depicted within global popular media as representative of this sort of nostalgic future of 'globalization' and its associated fears and promises. In cafes and restaurants in Xiamen, discussions about how 'we are witnessing an important global change taking place' (male, 48, England) and 'we are a part of history' (male, 26, the Netherlands) were common. These perceptions of China as symbolic of economic potential and the future of globalization were relevant for those who chose to leave home to spend time in Xiamen to help their social and economic progress back home. The following example demonstrates how postmodern 'rootless individualism' and short-term flexibility, rather than a 'condition' of postmodernity, are part of a process of long-term stability and solidarity exemplified through the construction of notions of time and place as commodities for later social exchange in another time and place.

Spending time: Emile

Before leaving his home town in regional France, Emile finished his MBA with a major in Chinese language and culture. He was one of a handful of interviewees who had an academic history and interest in China before arriving in Xiamen. This interest, though, was a preconceived and strategic method to enhance his career prospects in France itself, rather than any plans for settling in China on a long-term basis:

> My expectation is that … OK, I am in China but you don't know what is the future about something like this [*sic*]. I want to have five years' experience at least in China. Because now, if you want to have a job, if you don't have five years' experience in China people don't look at you. Just get your diploma and no experience … not enough. So five years' experience, learning to speak Chinese – maybe not specialized but learning to deal about some things about business and things like that, then I get to do whatever I want. I do the five years – that's the way life is. You have to have a job, you have to buy food. China is where everyone is looking now and if you don't have the time here and the experience then someone else will and you won't get the job.

Others, like Emile, also spoke about the decision to leave home as a decision aimed at improving their life-story back home. Some, though, also discussed their disappointment in the reality of achieving such aspirations. One young female interviewee from the United States said:

> The only reason I stayed here so long and worked so hard was because I thought it would help me when I went home … so I went home eventually and looked for work and my experience in China did not help at all. China means nothing on your CV but I didn't know that when I decided to come here and spend so much time here.

For this Xiamener, the perception that time in China would hold meaning elsewhere (at home in the West) was a motivational pull for the decision to leave home. The anticipated social capital that was to come with time in China did not produce the desired outcomes, yet the initial decision to leave was framed in terms of the 'promise' and 'expectation' of China as holding value as the future of globalism.

Time and place were constructed by Emile and others in Xiamen as an exchange that would be worth social or economic value back home. Knowledge of Chinese language, culture and customs for many was not as important as the *time* spent in this *place*.

This exploration of the lived realities of globalism and the decisions that people in Xiamen made to leave their homeland shows that time and place were a system of currency and commodity that would be exchanged for social or economic status back home at a later date. The previous example of 'short-termism' could be seen as potentially contradictory with notions of 'accumulation of time and place'. However, this apparent contradiction raises an important point about the relationship between time, place and global mobility. Both of these examples demonstrate that the 'rootless cosmopolitan' who values individualism and the short term exists in relationship with notions of long-termism, thick solidarity and the place-bound idea of 'home'. A further example of the long-termness of home is represented below by those who felt that this time spent here, in Xiamen, meant the perceived stopping of time back home which would resume upon return.

Suspending time and place

The great majority of Westerners in Xiamen spoke about the decision to leave home as a desire for 'time out' from an otherwise routine life-path. This perception of time stopping at home and resuming upon return was a theme throughout many interviews with people of different lengths of stay in Xiamen – even those who had been in Xiamen for a relatively long period of time (more than three years). Cohen (2003), in his study of European backpackers in Asia, also described 'travellers from affluence' as perceiving their trip as a 'break' or a 'time bubble'. He further described the irony inherent in this 'time out' from the pursuit of an ordinary career as a means to delay or halt the passage of time 'in the real world' of home, rather than a quest for an alternative way of life. Many Xiameners likewise felt a sense that they were suspending time at home and 'creating' their own time which promoted a process of personal growth and development – one of the principal life-goals of modern individualistic Western society (Cohen 1973: 105).

For some, time was suspended at what was perceived to be a crucial turning point in terms of individual biography. Death in the family, divorce, serious illness and job retrenchment led to making a decision to leave home in order to 'escape' the consequences of the future back home. For some, time in China would allow for a 'break from time and place' and served as a means to suspend the responsibilities of a personal dilemma.

Crisis managers: Craig and Roger

Craig arrived in Xiamen 18 months ago and I met him soon after his arrival at a Western restaurant popular with expatriates and business people. He arrived in the city with plans to stay for a few months. At the time of speaking with him, he worked for a Chinese trading firm with offices across North America and Europe and had bought a property in Xiamen with ocean views. Craig had a heart attack when he was 40 and sold the multi-million dollar business he had built from scratch to his son for a mere fraction of its worth. His decision to come to Xiamen was to escape what he perceived as a time shortage in his life. By coming to Xiamen, his time seemed to be more valuable, whereas had he stayed home time would have continued along its inevitably destructive course. By deciding to leave home, Craig was hoping to suspend the course of time back home:

> I had a heart attack when I was 40. That kind of changed my life. I decided that I wasn't going to work as much as I did. I was spending my money a lot more and a lot faster because you could be gone tomorrow... If you work hard, you can play hard, and that's the way I look at it. After the heart attack I said, life's too short. I got a wake-up call. I mean, I still smoke, obviously, but I did quit there for two, three years and I was on a health kick. It opened me up to saying hey, do something. I've travelled a lot since then.

Oliver's (2007, 2008) studies into retirement migrants or 'snowbirds' also report that migration is used as an opportunity to wipe clean past mistakes and even ties and commitments. For Benson and O'Reilly (2009b), lifestyle migrants from the West often present their decision to leave home in relation to a watershed event such as a redundancy or bereavement. This role of crisis in making the decision to leave home is an active means to reassert control over one's life-path. Time, or the repercussions of an action or event, in this sense, is perceived to 'stop' with regard to home and picks up in the new location. In contrast to retirement or leisure migrants, however, this did not necessarily equate to moving in order to build an alternative way of life. Instead, it did equate to moving in order to have a sense of the stopping of the progress of time back home. This factor in the decision-making process was a desire to keep life in a holding pattern until decisions about the future are made, or consequences of a trauma have passed.

Roger suffered a traumatic event that led to his decision to leave home. After being retrenched from the company he had worked with for 20 years and divorcing the mother of his two children he felt that his life in Canada was daunting and that he could no longer achieve the expectations for his life there. The decision to leave home was a response to this crisis and aimed towards suspending the social pressures, responsibilities and expectations of the future at home. Time for Roger would be suspended until he decided to return:

> I worked for a logistics company in Canada before I came here. The company I worked for, unfortunately, went into bankruptcy... I had been in that industry for 30 years. 20 years in that company. It wasn't a big decision at all. The company allowed me to make a lot of money, allowed me to make the change... They helped me make a decision. If the job was still going, the company still going, I would probably still be there. It was a good job, a good career. So I probably wouldn't have left. I wouldn't have even started doing what I am doing. Not at all.

> I only planned on going to China for one year but I've only been home once since I've been here – and that's almost five years now. When I was home I just wanted to come back. After two weeks I just didn't feel right. I thought, I want to go back. Everybody back home just seemed like they are just going through the motions. There was nothing new; they were just drifting through their lives. I'm not saying that's what it was but that's just the feeling I had. I didn't feel comfortable around that anymore... It was back to what it was that I wanted to get away from... Nothing's new. Nothing's challenging. I wasn't learning anything anymore. I was back to that rut.

Roger initially left home as a response to a perceived crisis. He felt that by leaving he could essentially suspend the consequences of time until he returned. However, when he returned home he felt that home represented the mundane, the long term ('Nothing's new, they were just drifting through their lives', 'I was back to that rut'). He was experiencing the emotional structure of anxiety ('That's just the *feeling* I had.

I didn't *feel comfortable* around that anymore. It was back to what it was that I wanted to get away from'). For Roger, time in Xiamen was a chance to escape the long-termness of home. Rather than a freely moving rootless cosmopolitan who chooses to live a short-term, flexible life, Roger chose to 'become global' as a *reaction to* the long term and to the anomic tension he experienced at home.

Craig and Roger both made the decision to leave home as a response to a crisis. Time spent in Xiamen was seen as a means to escape time at home. The relationship between time and home meant that for them time *there* stopped still and remained constant, while *here*, now, they could reassess and revalue their lives free of the structures and norms of home. The connections between short-termism and the long term and the use of place lead to a differently conceptualized notion of place, rather than its demise as a meaningful social category.

Time out: Jess and Cindy

Four of the people I interviewed and several I interacted with in Xiamen were between university and career and were taking what they described as a 'gap year' abroad – an increasingly popular rite of passage for many young and relatively affluent people from the West (see Clarke 2005; O'Reilly 2006; Hugo 2006; Patty 2011; Plomlin 2001).

During their stay in Xiamen they hoped they would find a sense of life or career 'direction' and be able to more clearly make the best career move when they eventually return home. Home, in this sense, is also perceived as stable and constant in the narratives of those who entered this 'time bubble'. They saw themselves as mobile, flexible and changing, unlike the people, cultures and institutions at 'home'.

Jess and Cindy were in their early 20s and from southern England. They had both graduated from top-class universities in the last six months and had been in Xiamen for less than four months. They were teaching English at a Chinese high school for a small allowance and living in the outer suburbs of Xiamen. I interviewed them together in a tea-house near the university.

Jess summed up her situation thus:

> I sort of thought it would broaden my horizons and it sort of challenges yourself to live in a different country. With different ways of doing stuff. And I didn't have any idea about what I wanted to do at home. I thought I might go home with more of an idea. You find out what you want from life more when you're in a place like this.

Cindy corroborated this sense of 'time out':

> I don't know what I will do when I get back. Part of the reason for coming was that it will give me a year to find what I wanted to do. I don't know. A lot of people go abroad before university but I think because the whole getting jobs thing is so non-stop once you're into it, I think there's a temptation to say, well, before I do that I'll go to China or travel. There is a feeling that once you're in the system it's hard to get out.

For Jess and Cindy, their 'real lives' and career paths were waiting for them back home in the future. But for now, here in Xiamen, they could use this time to decide and reconsider their identity, ambition and values. Jess and Cindy were yet to become ideal flexible workers, but thought that once they did develop their skills back home, they would find it difficult to escape the demands of the workplace and of community expectations.

This context of heightened individualism and short-termism is again seen in tension with the expectations of the community and the long term. Their time in Xiamen was allowing them time to develop their notion of individualism (that is, what do *I* want to do with *my* life? Where will *I* go? How will *my* biography unfold?) without the social constraints and 'pressures' of home. Their decision to leave home, while prior to the beginning of their careers, was also a performance of the emotional structure of anxiety in the sense that it also indicated a tension between individualism and community expectations and structures.

Elsrud (1998) also found that time was perceived to stop, or be left behind, for the Swedish female backpackers she studied. Elsrud claimed that 'one of the things they claim they left behind to a large extent was clock-time... Travelling as "time out" is found when we focus on travel as a withdrawal from clock-time and from routines of everyday life' (Elsrud 1998: 311). This withdrawal from clock-time and routine associated with a different place is shown in the following chapter to contribute to a sense of freedom from the structure and boundaries of home.

Each of the people described in this section perceived themselves as physically and mentally distanced from the everyday structures of home. 'Time out' in this sense is closely related to 'liminality', a concept used to characterize periods in between different structures as well as the time away from home in the pilgrim's quest for spiritual centres

(Turner 1969). The decision to leave home in the West for China was a performance of the use and manipulation of time and place in order to rectify anomic tensions between the value of individualism and the paradoxical experience of community and social structure. The three themes discussed here (the cult of short-termism; the accumulation of time and place; and the suspension of time and place) are interrelated and all point towards the simultaneous production of localized, personal emotional structure of anxiety *and* the context of globalism manifested in the value of individualism.

Conclusion

The middling migrant from the West should be understood in far more complex terms than as merely top-down bearers of structural forces of economic globalization. The localized experience of an anomic tension between the value of individualism and the expectations of the community led to the decision of many participants to leave home. Accounts of the lived-experience of this tension demonstrate that the moral landscape of global mobility is a contextualized process, rather than a condition of 'rootlessness' and ambivalence caused by globalization. The construction of time as short term was seen to take place in relation to what was perceived as the 'long-termness' of home. Rather than the globalist value of individualism resulting in 'thin' social structure and a demise of place as a meaningful social category (Turner and Rojek 2001), these accounts of leaving the West for Xiamen were evidence of the continued relevance of 'thick' forms of social structure whereby place and time were used in order to rectify perceived structural tensions.

Claims that globalism is resulting in the demise of place, structure and emotion as meaningful categories of sociality can therefore be brought into question. The motivations people gave for the reasons they left their homeland for China uncover how people position themselves between the values of individualism and the values of the community. The resulting vulnerability was expressed here as the emotional structure of anxiety. Rather than 'coming to China' many in Xiamen were in fact moving 'away from' the structures of their homeland.

Individualism is a value which underpins globalism and exists alongside notions of the short term and non-commitment. 'Home', however, was a temporally situated moral landscape which was produced in relation to the present place (Xiamen). In other words, home represented the Other of individualism: stability, mundanity, commitment and progressive time. For many in Xiamen, the decision to move was a means to palliate the anomic tension or sense of precariousness (or vulnerability) felt between this individualism and the experience of being an outsider in terms of the workplace and in terms of identity and belonging. The decision to leave was an active decision made to rectify and resist these tensions and thus adds a focus on agency and context to Beck's (2000) suggestions that personal insecurity and vulnerability are the consequences of wider economic and structural globalism.

Theories that suggest that place or territoriality is diminishing in significance for transnational skilled workers (Robinson 2004; Zukin 1991) can also be brought into question. The decision to leave home does not signal an end to the significance of the place of home. Rather, the decision to leave for another place is a profoundly personal expression of the moral landscape of home. The meanings associated with the move to Xiamen are performed and understood in relation to this place known as 'home'. The relevance and the meaning of place remain powerful within social action *because* the Xiamener is away. These stories are stories of territoriality, of home and of what these concepts mean for those living transnational lives.

It is important to note here that the experiences of those who left the West were social and the narratives of those in Xiamen that recounted the decision to leave were inevitably moral. That is, these narratives of decision-making situated the self within a normative background and structure. These narratives point towards social and contextual values, aims, orientations, expectations and choices. In other words, rather than free-floating and increasingly 'de-structured' cosmopolitans, the decisions to leave home were made within a context bounded by conflicting value structures and were an agentic reaction against, as well as legitimation of, such value structures. These structural contexts were associated with place. The Xiameners used places and the decision to move geographically as a means to palliate the tensions experienced in the moral landscape of home. Place, structure and emotion are hence shown here to be intricately linked and relevant within the lives of global transnational workers.

Time and place were key conceptual indicators for how people placed themselves within this context of individualization and globalism. Time and place were being used and manipulated by many Westerners in Xiamen in order to appease tensions or crises 'back home'. It is the suspension of notions of time and place and their reconstruction that lead us to understand contemporary global transnationalism as ritual. After making the decision to leave the place and the time known as 'home',

Xiamen became a liminal site. It is within this site that was freedom is realized, allowing for a period of creativity and re-imagining of the life-courses, values and structures of both home and away.

The decision to leave home for Xiamen was the personal, concrete and localized form of the large abstraction described here as globalism. It was also a parallel manifestation of the global consequences of the values and tensions inherent in the postmodern hyper-inflated value of individualism. It was in the making of this decision that experiences of time and place were challenged, enhanced and restructured (Elsrud 1998: 310). This perspective adds further agency to Beck's claims that globalism results in personal insecurity and vulnerability. Even before leaving, 'home' was seen as a moral construction of order and structure. The journey to Xiamen was a means of challenging, escaping or re-conceptualizing this structure.

3
Ecstasy and Freedom

As newcomers in an unfamiliar environment, Western transnational workers underwent a period akin to Victor Turner's (1969) notion of 'liminality'. Anthropologists such as Turner have used this concept to focus on a certain state experienced by people as they pass over a threshold from one stage of life to another. During the liminal stage, or the 'between' stage, a person's status becomes ambiguous; they are neither 'here nor there' but are between all fixed points of classification. Thus the form and rules of both the person's earlier state and the person's state to come are suspended.

Recent studies into privileged migration have noted this experience of liminality which forms an important part of the migratory experience (see, for example, Trundle 2009). I argue that what is interesting is not necessarily liminality itself but the way that this phase sets the scene for active reconsidering of social structure. It is the uncertainty of this stage that allows for the path to be paved for fundamental transformations of identities and community.

Postmodern theory claims that globalized society is characterized by a sense of vulnerability. Theorists such as Beck (1999, 2000), Bauman (1995, 2000, 2006, 2007) and Bryan Turner (2000) conceptualize this vulnerability as a sense of precariousness and instability which, they argue, results from globalism. The side effects, according to these theorists, are the erosion of social structure, place and emotion in meaningful social action.

The arrival exists in a state of vulnerability characterized here as 'ecstasy'. These liminal Xiameners are vulnerable because they are on the threshold of an unfamiliar social structure and for now are without the stability and certainty of 'home'. Liminality therefore points to a relationship with social structures.

Liminality also points to a relationship with notions of place. The term 'liminality' has been primarily used within the field of anthropology to describe a rite of passage or a ritual. According to Appadurai (1996), a great deal of what has been termed rites of passage are concerned with the production of what we might call *local* subjects – actors who properly belong to a situated community of kin, neighbours, friends or enemies (Appadurai 1996). The concept of a liminal rite of passage can be applied to skilled transnational workers in order to explore the process by which these mobile people begin to produce localized contexts and structured communities.

While anthropological literature has tended to use the concept of the rite of passage to refer to spiritual quests within traditional societies, these concepts are applied here to the transformations of self and community within a contemporary globalized setting. In this way, the experience of participating in global practices can be seen as a ritual aimed at legitimating the moral landscape of this globalism (manifested here through the values of individualism, freedom and difference). The result of this is a reconstruction and reconsidering of social structure, identity and community in a localized context.

The Xiameners' contemporary journeys can be likened to a pilgrimage – a transformative journey or quest for something considered sacred. Here, the transformations taking place occur as the Xiameners reflect upon and reconsider the moral landscape of home. In this context the sacred is globalism itself. The journey of contemporary mobility is conducted within a structured moral landscape and, like a pilgrimage, leads to a reaffirmation of the values that underpin solidarity. In this case, the values or 'beliefs' that are reaffirmed or legitimated through the journey are those underpinning global mobility, such as individualism, freedom and difference.

The modern value of 'freedom' can be used to explore this transformative process further. Through using the emotional structure of 'ecstasy' as a lens through which to analyse the interview data, the process of reconstructing and legitimating the value of freedom becomes visible. The term 'ecstasy' originates from the Greek *ekstasis* meaning to stand outside oneself or to be displaced. Standing free of familiar symbols of status and culture, free of the past and the future and within an illegible urban environment, liminal Xiameners are, for the moment, displaced. They are outside of themselves in terms of identities and communities which they belonged to in the past and might belong to again in the future. Here the emotional structure of ecstasy is understood to be a *social* experience which exists as part of a structured rite of passage leading towards the legitimation of the values that underpin global mobilities.

Notions of time and place can be seen as conceptual markers around which to understand the motivations for leaving home. Similarly, new understandings of time and place upon arrival in Xiamen allowed for a process of liminality and transformation to occur. A profound sense of freedom from the constraints of the time (past experiences and future obligations and responsibilities) and place (the landscape and culture) known as 'home' were evident in most interviews.

Freedom from time and place

We have seen how time and place were used by transnational workers in order to resolve a sense of anomic tension between individualism and the expectations of the community when making the decision to leave home. Upon arrival in Xiamen, concepts of time and place are further repositioned. Once in a setting that is culturally and geographically distanced from home, those I spoke to in Xiamen expressed a sense of *freedom*. This freedom was contrasted with the perceived constraints of the past in terms of personal histories, experiences and careers and the future in terms of norms, responsibilities and obligations.

Once in Xiamen, previous cultural signifiers of identity, social rank and structure were stripped of the social meanings they held in the past. Likewise, markers of rank and structure in the future did not yet apply. The liminal transnational existed within the present during this phase as networks of classifications that normally locate their positions within social and cultural space were absent. This sense of freedom from the past and the future allowed the liminal Xiamener to experience a period of creativity and reflection. Here, the focus is on the initial period of liminality before reflection allowed for new boundaries and rules of group inclusion and exclusion.

Concepts of 'place' were also repositioned after arrival in Xiamen. The illegibility of a culturally and linguistically different urban environment led Xiameners to experience a period of being a stranger on more than one front. In other words, the Xiamener was an outsider with regard to their home society, as well as the host society. It was in the process of deciphering the local environment and reconsidering concepts of home, nation and social structure that identity and community were renegotiated.

Turner also referred to liminality as social anti-structure (Turner 1969). This anti-structure is composed of human bonds that exist outside the structure of roles, statuses and positions within society, such as status and hierarchy (Turner 1969). However, the bonds that exist during the liminal period are constructed in relation to a form of 'thick solidarity', albeit a solidarity which for the present is weakened. In order to emphasize the continued relevance of social structure within this time of being on the margins, I prefer to use the term liminality.

Upon arriving in Xiamen and faced with cultural, linguistic and urban differences, those I spoke with became aware that what is considered common sense at home no longer appears to be so. The understood, expected and familiar social signifiers and rules of interaction no longer seem to apply. Xiameners spoke about this experience of freedom from the structure of time and place as freedom from the everyday certainties of home.

Death and taxes

Sweating with the intense summer humidity of Xiamen, Emile sits at an outdoor plastic table sipping a cold beer. While we talk, children approach us begging for money, or, at the least, the empty bottle which they can hope to sell for its glass. Emile waves them off and keeps drinking. At the shady table next to us, a group of old men drink tea and gamble with small wooden blocks in a game that appears to Emile and I like a cross between dominos and poker. I ask him about the benefits of life in Xiamen and being away from France:

> You don't have to worry about your taxes. You don't have to worry about your loans. You don't have to worry about…well, anything from there. So it's easy. I don't have a link. Sometimes I wonder how the government is making any money actually. Everybody is here and nobody is paying taxes! There is less responsibility here…I'll get old sometime, sure. It happens. But I don't think about it right now. Maybe I could be a millionaire, but I don't care about it right now.

For Emile and others, the obligations of the past – of home – were no longer relevant upon arrival in Xiamen. Similarly, the responsibilities of the future, of age and maturity at home, no longer applied. We have seen how this notion of suspending time was a motivation for leaving home in the West. As the journey continues those in Xiamen experienced a sense of living for the present. Michael, from the United Kingdom, explained this experience from his perspective:

> Besides the financial reasons, I am glad I am away from family pressure about getting a 'real job', you know? And did I waste my degree…that kind of thing. But I think there is plenty of time for

> that in the future...I do get a bit of family pressure and also financial pressure back home. I certainly don't miss that.

Financial pressure, family expectations and the ramifications of career and educational choices no longer seemed to apply to many Xiameners. Many also spoke of a sense of freedom from the media, politics and information of home. For example, Roger (54, Canada) stated:

> I know this sounds silly, but at home in Canada you get information to death! I mean it! TV, radio, newspapers...it's a constant bombardment. You get annoyed. What I like here is that I don't have that information if I don't want it. There's no television station that gives me anywhere near the information they have at home...It's keeping it simple.

Others spoke about this freedom from 'information' and freedom from keeping 'up to date' with politics and national and international affairs. Another respondent, a 27-year-old Australian male said:

> My interest in things in the 'real world' has changed since I've been here. Before, I was interested in politics, trying to get to know who to vote for...I tried to get involved with these things. Now, very little. I find it more funny than interesting.

This sense of freedom from information was often linked to a changing political awareness. While theories of cosmopolitanism suggest that skilled transnational workers would increasingly connect to global issues and develop an awareness of 'humanity' as a whole, in Xiamen contrasting evidence was found. During this liminal ecstatic stage, most people I interviewed suggested that their relationship to global media and information had changed since being in Xiamen towards increasing disconnection. Many enjoyed a sense of 'freedom' from information. Some recounted enjoying the ability to now 'choose' (male, 58, New Zealand) which information they received and when they liked, rather than the 'constant bombardment of information' (male, 27, Australia) they said they received at home.

Discourses on globalization are often linked to the flows of technology which make possible increasing dissemination of information and culture (Appadurai 1996). Nevertheless, this research shows that skilled transnational workers, rather than necessarily engaging with such technology and information, also recounted a reaction against such processes in their day-to-day lives. Rather than top-down bearers of the multiple processes of globalization, skilled transnational workers from the West were involved in contextualized constructions of what it meant to be 'global' at the local level, which did not always result in the acceptance of global technologies and information connectivity. Rather, many recounted a sense of 'freedom' from information and politics.

This sense of freedom from media-saturated national and global politics can be related to the notion of cosmopolitan ambivalence, which is described by theorists such as Beck (2006) and Turner (2000) to be a consequence of increasingly mobile lives. In expressing a sense of freedom from information and politics, these Xiameners were also expressing a form of this ambivalence. The interviewees often articulated a form of this ambivalence which they claimed not to feel when at home.

However, this sense of freedom from place and time is part of a much larger journey. At this point, we note only that ambivalence could be seen as a stage of the journey. Later we will see that this ambivalence contributes to the later renegotiation or reconstruction of relatively 'thick' forms of community and attachment. It is this experience of being outside of home, of being for a time in a state of ambivalence and disconnection, which allows for the later creation and maintenance of social structure at the local level. The postmodern 'rootless' and ambivalent cosmopolitan exists as a part of a larger journey which is embedded within place, structure and emotional experience.

The experience of being away from the media and information, disconnected from political issues and away from the responsibilities and expectations of family and work, can be understood as a sense of ecstatic (or liminal) freedom. The meanings of the past and the future no longer seemed to apply. This sense of freedom was heightened and reinforced by those in Xiamen using metaphors commonly associated with liminality (Turner 1969) – invisibility, anonymity, childhood, invalidity and the wilderness.

Invisibility and anonymity

Upon arrival in Xiamen, Westerners felt a sense of freedom from the structures and norms of home. Faced with cultural difference, the Xiameners were led to an awareness that rules of social interaction and signifiers of status and identity at home no longer seemed to hold the same meaning. During this period, common sense became visible and hence questionable.

As a result, signifiers of identity and 'belonging' also no longer seemed to apply upon arrival in Xiamen. Accents and regional dialects, family histories, friendships, cultural tastes and fashions did not hold the meanings attached to them back home. Aguilar (1999: 121) described the centrality of the stripping of social signifiers for the liminal process: 'The first point about liminality is that it's not just some vague in-between state; it is, rather, a very specific kind of in-between state – the kind that involves the stripping away of one's socially identifying features.' Markers of status and identity were thus seen to belong in the past. Arriving in Xiamen, the Westerner was akin to a 'man-without-history' (Schutz 1944). In other words, they were *strangers* (Simmel [1900] 1978).

Farrer's (2010: 1212) study of Westerners living in Shanghai describes Western expatriates as 'a special category of strangers within a Chinese city' which he claims represent an ideal base to question narratives of cosmopolitan citizenship. I suggest that what Farrer is perhaps implying is that this particular version of strangerhood is 'special' because it is experienced on two fronts. Not only did the Xiameners feel they were outsiders in China, but they also felt like outsiders among other Westerners who did not necessarily understand the significance of the social signifiers of home. New arrivals in Xiamen were experiencing what Aguilar (1999) termed 'double liminality'. That is, they were on the margins not only of the structures of the host society but also of the structures of home.

The liminal period hence involves a complex relationship between the home and the host. The perception of being free from social structure is reinforced and legitimated through the experience of being an 'outsider' within China. An interviewee from the United States described this experience by saying that 'there is always that sense that this is not your home, this is not your background'. The sense of freedom from the structures of home was constantly reinforced through this awareness of the new status as an outsider in China. Knowing that they needn't follow the norms of here (China) or there (home), the Xiameners felt invisible and anonymous.

Upon arrival in Xiamen, the experience of strangerhood was linked to these feelings of invisibility and anonymity. Stripped of the social signifiers of home and the related freedom from time and place, Xiameners often experienced a sense of being distanced from the social gaze of home (Foucault 1975). It was in the perception that no one from 'home' could literally 'see' them and therefore potentially contribute to the regulation of their behaviour according to their accepted norms that led to this sense of 'freedom'. The lack of the social context of home meant that the Xiamener, as a stranger, felt unknown and to some degree unknowable in this setting. A 45-year-old Canadian teacher said:

> No one knows anything about you here and you don't have to tell
> them. People want to know where you come from first of all but
> people don't really talk about their lives at home. None of it matters
> to anyone here.

The stranger was anonymous – an individual's past and their identity
were unknown to those they interact with. As a result of this perceived
freedom the after-effects of action no longer appeared to apply as much
during this liminal phase.

Aguilar's (1999: 119) study of Filipino migrant workers described a
similar experience of social invisibility of the internationally mobile:

> The international labour migrant's social and spatial dislocation
> transports the worker into a temporal limbo of sorts. Without a past,
> the migrant contract worker also has no future there . . . His/her sense
> of place has no fixity and the worker joins other labour migrants
> in constituting a category of people who, betwixt and between in
> the structural position they occupy relative to the local population's
> conception of that society, are collectively marginalized into social
> invisibility.

Unlike Aguilar's migrant contract workers, the skilled Western transnationals I spoke to in Xiamen considered themselves as actively choosing
this time of this 'temporal limbo'. Rather than considering themselves marginalized or bound by restrictions (whether bureaucratic or
cultural), the Xiameners saw themselves as freer from such restrictions than they would be at home. The difference between Aguilar's
migrant workers and those I interviewed was one of perceived agency
and led to freedom being experienced through the emotional structure of ecstasy. Like Aguilar's migrant workers, however, the Xiameners
were also experiencing a similar process of perceived 'invisibility', reinforced by a local urban environment which they found difficult to
decipher.

Constantly aware of their dual status as an outsider in the place they
are living, and an outsider from the place they had come from, those
I spoke to in Xiamen often used metaphors associated with liminal
processes, such as the child and the invalid.

The child and the invalid

Skilled transnational Westerners in Xiamen often spoke about the experience of grappling with strangerhood and double liminality as a time of
constantly questioning and trying to understand what they previously

had believed was common sense, such as everyday routines and public safety. The stranger was hence someone who Schutz (1944: 4) described as 'essentially the man who has to place into question nearly everything that seems to be unquestionable to the members of the approached group'. This deciphering of the everyday was often likened to being like that of a child or an invalid.

For David (30, UK), this experience was something he enjoyed:

> Not speaking the language and not understanding is part of the excitement for me. I can't think of anything that excites the imagination more than to be totally like a three year old again. Wondering around. Nearly getting run over. Can't write. Can't speak. That's cool, you know? It's such an experience! I want to do it again!

David likened the experience of being in an illegible landscape to being like a small child. Daily routines were difficult for him to accomplish. For David and the others described here, this experience was something he felt a sense of excitement – or ecstasy – experiencing.

Others also described this process of learning and comprehending daily routines while in Xiamen. According to Bethany (26, US):

> At home, everything is so easy. You know what to expect. When you go to buy a stamp or a loaf of bread, you know what will happen and how to go about things. But here, even the smallest task becomes difficult. You realize that buying a stamp is not the same everywhere and you never know what will happen.

Faced with illegible everyday social practice, the liminal Xiamener was forced to question the universality of basic social 'rules' at home. Just weeks after my own initial arrival in China in 2002, I was told the following anecdote by an English-teaching colleague from Canada:

> At home, you go to bed believing that black is black and white is white. In China, you wake up and realize that here these people see that black is white, and white is black. I then spend my entire day trying to convince myself to see it the way they do: that black is *not* black. It is white.

Such metaphors used to explain the questioning of 'thinking-as-usual' were commonly used by Westerners.

For others, like Roger, being a stranger was described as stressful:

The first year here was great. Literally, my first year here I was an invalid. I was free of being a father and a family member. It was stressful. Is that weird? Don't get me wrong, it was great. It was a step. I was doing something new. You don't have to deal with your problems.

Here Roger was stating that the new sense of freedom he experienced involved freedom from his previous social roles (as father and partner). Despite feeling stressed, he also experienced a sense of excitement. This ecstatic liminality was linked to the perception that he was progressing in terms of developing his own individual biography – it was a 'step' and he was 'doing something new'. Roger's journey was simultaneously away from past structure and one of personal achievement.

This experience of ecstatic liminality was linked to the perceived cultural differences in the everyday landscape of Xiamen. This deciphering of the unfamiliar and interpreting of difference eventually form the basis for the reconstitution of structure and community in Xiamen. However, in order for this restructuring to occur, the Xiamener necessarily experienced a sense of being between the structures of time and place, a phenomenon that can be described as 'strangerhood'. Such strangerhood was characterized by a questioning of the fundamental rules and taken-for-grantedness of both the home and the host society.

If I was to stop this discussion of global mobility and solidarity at this point of liminality, then the 'rootless' postmodern and cosmopolitan theories of identities would be an accurate depiction of reality. Indeed, the Xiameners experienced a sense of ambivalence and weakening of social structure. However, this snapshot approach tends to universalize a particular situation and neglects the larger contextual journey. This liminal stage in fact represents an essential precursor to the reconstitution of notions of place and structure.

It is through the challenges of what has been termed here 'double liminality' that both the contributions and contradictions of the values underpinning globalism and the localized experience of structure and community become apparent. To achieve this transformation through this journey, the individual undergoes a period stripped of the symbols which locate her within cultural space.

The wilderness

The metaphor of 'living in the wilderness' or 'on the frontier' was often used to explain this experience. Within Xiamen, this metaphor took on a particular relevance associated with the rapidly evolving urban landscape and was eventually to be implicated in the structuring and negotiation of a localized and contextualized community.

Between the high-rise apartment blocks and chaotic traffic of Xiamen, are hidden a maze of tiny laneways wide enough only for a bicycle and small enough to be lost within. Michael and I wander through them, past the remnants of communal housing, the smell of incense and street sellers with baskets of unidentifiable fruit. A bicycle passes us with a refrigerator tied precariously to the back and carrying a baby on the front. As we walk through the unnamed laneways, I ask Michael about how he finds life in Xiamen:

> It's part of the attraction of staying … not knowing … I mean, I don't understand this place. It makes it interesting. Within the first year, if I could speak the language, within the next year I probably would have decided, well, there's nothing new for me here. I won't leave till I know what's going on around me … Humans can adjust to almost any environment we have to. When I first came here you couldn't get coffee, cheese, you could only get sweet bread, not salty bread. You can live with that. You can survive on that. Now you can get these things, but there was a time when it was harder.

Many who had been in Xiamen for more than one year spoke about 'doing time roughing it' in China. Stories of life without the comforts of the West – often spoken about in terms of food or commodities – were common. This period of hardship was to later form divisions within the community as people distanced themselves from or connected to others who had likewise placed value on such times spent without the 'comforts' of home. However, the period of liminal ecstasy was often associated with tales of hardship or 'roughing it' without the common familiar 'necessities' of home.

Stories of deciphering the city were sometimes spoken about in terms of navigating a 'frontier' or the 'wild' environment. This sentiment echoes Iyer's (2001: 295) claim that '[i]n our global urban context, [being in a foreign land] is an equivalent to living in the wilderness'. The experience of the city as a dangerous wilderness was often a contrast for interviewees who had witnessed the rapid change within the city. According to Michael:

> The place is just changing. I feel like I am in the Wild West, you know? You're on the frontier. You ride the horse and nothing ever gets clear because it's just moving all the time.

The increasing traffic on the roads in Xiamen was frequently discussed as the manifestation of this fear of a changing and indecipherable urban environment. The perceived chaos in the urban environment contributed to this sense of being on the margins of familiarity and structure for liminal Xiameners. For example:

> The traffic in general, whether its foot, pedals or vehicular. It's all a lack of…of…order. Because we see it. It's order. It really is. The disorder is also something I like about China, though. I like the fact that it's different. I don't like the fact that it's dangerous while it's different though.
>
> (Male, 52, Canada)

This journey through the urban 'wilderness' was constructed as one of achievement among those who stayed on in Xiamen. Surviving the hardship of life without familiarity, with incomprehension and uncertainty was an achievement that we later see forms the basis for a system of hierarchy within the emerging Western community in Xiamen.

However, it was as an *individual* that the Western 'pilgrim' must initially function, before reaching an elevated position later in the journey. They must go through this period of sacrifice, self-denial and the abandonment of what are perceived as worldly (or familiar) comforts and pleasures in order to later re-engage with community. The ecstasy of being of being outside of the structures and familiarity of home is experienced simultaneously with this heightened sense of individualism. This journey provides the necessary context for the reflexive legitimation of the moral landscape of global mobility and the values which underpin it (such as individualism, freedom and difference). The journey of achievement described here is only possible due to this liminal stage outside of previously taken-for-granted social structures and without the social signifiers of home and the local social environment.

In this liminal context, the transnational Xiamener was engaged in a process of the negation of self in order to recover the self at a later stage. This negation was expressed using the metaphors of the invisible, the anonymous, the child, the invalid and the wilderness. This ritual journey of self-transformation led to the reconsideration of the moral landscape of globalism. Upon arrival in Xiamen, Westerners spoke about being free from the constraints of time and place and about the journey through an indecipherable and sometimes hostile urban environment. The Xiameners, in this liminal stage, can be seen as vulnerable; that is, they were in a period of 'positioning the self' between the emotional structure of freedom and the awareness of a contrasting social constraint at home. In this way, the value of freedom, which is seen in this book as one of the values underpinning globalism (see Figure 1), is always constructed within a localized context. The moral landscape of globalism, therefore, is reconstituted in the ways people experience and define themselves in relation to place, structure and emotion.

'Writing your own rules'

This perceived negation of self and break from structure allowed the Xiameners to exhibit action which would be constrained at other times and places. All interviewees spoke openly and sometimes passionately about differing standards of behaviour that foreigners adopt upon arrival in Xiamen. The 'rules' that are often broken include the excessive consumption of alcohol, frequenting brothels or 'massage parlours' and nightclubs. Free of the constraints of home and away from the social gaze of community members, life could become somewhat hedonistic and ecstatic for liminal Xiameners.

Both Farrer's (2011) study of Westerners living in Shanghai and Walsh's (2007) study of British expatriates in Dubai reported nightlife and going out and consuming alcohol as more central to their lives when away from home. Similarly, participants in Xiamen described a permissive sexual atmosphere and excessive drinking associated with this holiday mentality.

Callum had arrived from Scotland two years before and ran the Chinese arm of a trading business. I met him and his partner for lunch in a Singaporean restaurant:

> Foreigners behave massively differently here than they do at home. We often talk about this. Everybody here behaves the way that they would if they were back home and they were on holiday in Spain for two weeks and it didn't matter, they could do anything that they wanted, they knew it was going to stay here and it didn't matter, it wouldn't effect anything else in their life. And so they go bananas. Everybody here thinks that they can get away with everything and anything and it doesn't matter.

The experience of double liminality – of belonging neither within the structures of home nor within that of the host society – reinforced and legitimated this behaviour. The obvious differences between the local urban environment and with home culture ensured that the consequences of actions for the Westerner no longer applied in the same way as they do for the local people (Farrer 2011; Walsh 2007). Sally, a 40-year-old Australian entrepreneur reflected:

> No one is going to say that you're not performing to society's books. You don't have to think about that. Because here you are a foreigner and Chinese people see you as being foreign anyway, so you don't have to worry about it. You're not conforming to *their* society. So you can write your own rules.

Sally's claim that in Xiamen 'you can write your own rules' resonates with Beck's argument that the heightened individualism of late modernity results in 'do-it-yourself-biographies' and postmodern claims that globalization is resulting in a rootless, ambivalent cosmopolitanism. However, such cosmopolitanism needs to be examined both within its local context and as a part of longer ongoing journeys.

For Sally, the difference she experienced in Xiamen led to a heightened awareness of her status as an outsider, and this awareness encouraged a lack of conformity with prevailing norms. The stranger was free from social discipline and lived without the regulatory function of a community or being embedded in a local social structure. During this liminal period, the lack of cohesive community binding allowed for social interaction and behaviour that would be considered inappropriate at other times and places. As Michael pointed out:

> Back home you are surrounded by people who will pull you into line for misbehaving. But here, who is going to do that? I've seen people go off the rails in China and talking to them doesn't seem to do much good ... Here, you are perhaps more isolated. You feel more isolated.

Cindy (23, England) echoed the feeling: 'Here you feel like you don't need to answer to anyone.' The experience of being socially unrecognizable – of being anonymous and invisible – freed time to break rules and live free from perceived restrictions. This was a time of *ecstasy*. Kathy from Canada said: 'China is like a big roller-coaster. You go from the highest of highs to the lowest of lows in 24 hours.' The experience of these emotional extremities (conceptualized here as ecstasy) was made possible through the experience of being on the margins of social structure – both the structures of home and the structures of Xiamen.

The socially structured nature of this ecstatic liminality can be shown through the varying degrees to which this was experienced by expatriates in Xiamen, depending on the degree to which the Westerner remained embedded within the structures and milieu of 'home'. Those who were recruited from home and were working in Xiamen within a familiar setting and who were employed with traditional expatriate packages (including top-quality Western-style housing – often in a security-gated complex and provided with daily assistance such as a driver, cook, maid and help with shopping and navigating the city) did not experience such extremes of emotion, nor did they employ metaphors of invisibility, anonymity, the child and the wilderness to the same degree as those who did not have access to familiar work and home settings upon arrival.

For example, Rhonda, a 32-year-old Australian and long-term Xiamener said:

> It's not like everyone goes crazy when they get here. I mean, some people go right off the rails but there's also people who don't. Usually the people who come here with their job and stay in [gated-security housing for foreigners]. They've got their families with them and they work in the same company as they did at home. So they don't really hit the town as much as people who came here on their own. I came here on my own as a teacher and those days were pretty mad. We just didn't live the Monday to Friday lifestyle. Every day was Friday night. But since I've been married and met lots of other kind of corporates and you see a different side to it. They don't go as much, you know, crazy when they arrive because they can't.

Rhonda was highlighting that the period of ecstatic liminality was possible for those who 'did not bring home with them' (in terms of family or workplace). Those that did 'bring home with them' were more bound by the social norms and boundaries of home than those who arrived on their own. Such distinctions between the experience of liminality and cultural difference eventually became the basis of emerging divisions and the restructuring of community. Here it is important to note that the liminal processes were experienced and recounted to different degrees depending on the initial relationship to structures and cultural patterns of home upon arrival in the city.

It was the transnational who arrived and worked on their own volition – as an individual – who was in a greater position to feel outside of the regulatory gaze and the structures of home. For the Xiameners, the performance of freedom was linked to the performance of individualism and the journey was a means to legitimate and reconsider this value structure. The liminal journey of achievement described here is an *individual* quest for self and identity within a communal context. It was, however, the common experience of what Turner (1969) termed 'anti-structure' that provided the basis for a unique form of unstructured togetherness with others undergoing the same process.

Communitas

Liminal Westerners in Xiamen daily negotiated an illegible city and were reminded of their status as strangers, perceived to be free from the constraints and the gaze of the place they had come from, and the place they were currently in. However, the ecstasy of stepping outside one's self was performed with others who were similarly undergoing the same processes and experiences of normlessness.

In his discussion on liminality, Turner (1969) described the existence of two major models for human interrelatedness which are juxtaposed and alternating. The first model was society as a structured, differentiated and often hierarchical system of politico-legal-economic positions with many types of evaluation 'separating men in terms of "more" or "less"' (Turner 1969: 360). The second model, which could be observed in the liminal period that many Xiameners experienced, is society as an unstructured or rudimentarily structured and relatively undifferentiated community of equal individuals (Turner 1969: 360). This second model Turner (1969: 371) termed *communitas* and he argued it emerges wherever social structure does not.

In Xiamen, many expressed themselves using liminal metaphors such as the child and the wilderness, and invisibility also spoke about the differing behaviour of Westerners who stepped outside the boundaries of previously familiar community, structure and identity. However, this liminal experience of 'stepping out' was often done together with others who were likewise undergoing such a liminal ritual.

The *communitas* was a form of community without hierarchy, rank or rules. On arrival in Xiamen, many transnationals developed friendships with other foreigners who would be considered to be in very different positions in the social hierarchies of home. For example, Jess (21, UK) explained:

> I probably wouldn't be friends with the people I have made friends with here if I had met them at home . . . we wouldn't have mixed in the same circles at all. We're completely different there. But here it's

nice to get to know each other. I don't know...you just get these stereotypes and you think you never would have met them but then you realize you get on quite well with them.

For Jess, membership of different social groupings at home no longer applied in Xiamen. As a result, she felt she could interact with people from different social subgroups more comfortably than she would within the structures of her home society. Simon also spoke about the contrasting friendship ties at home and in Xiamen between Westerners:

I don't necessarily think that the people I am friends with in China would be my friends if I met them back home. There are some who feel perhaps I wouldn't have sufficient enough in common to be friends with them back home, but the friendship dynamics are much different in China than they are in the West, in England.

In Xiamen, there was a shared experience or a bond that was perceived to be beyond such structural rankings. Kathy, a 52-year-old Canadian English teacher expressed the strength of this bond when she said:

You do have those things in common here. Something's been thrown at you to give you the desire and the courage to leave your country, and yes, you do share that here.

At this early liminal stage, these commonalities and this sense of social solidarity involved a perceived meeting of equals regardless of social ranking. The stripping of past signifiers of structure and freedom discussed earlier in this chapter allowed for the establishment of a common bond based on newly imagined connections with others. This notion of having a common bond was discussed in terms of a shared experience in having the 'courage' to leave home, or in 'coping' with the cultural difference of Xiamen, or of a shared history and background assumed by the category 'Westerner'. Frederik (26, the Netherlands) said:

It's like you can walk into any place and if you see another Westerner you can just start talking to them and it's not weird. At home that would be weird and you'd think, who is this guy? But here, you have something in common from the start. You are both *laowai* [foreign/Western] and you are both here, in this place and you have left home. It's like, you know this person must be dealing with Chinese people and all those things like renting houses and getting stuff done, you know? So you can just start talking. No problem. I love that. You meet some really interesting people here. It makes me think how we never just start talking to people at home.

By mere fact of being a co-foreigner in Xiamen, certain assumptions and connections were often made with others. Nigel (52, UK) reflected:

> What you have to understand is that those of us that choose to live in what is a strange place tend to be quite strong characters. Quite individualistic and probably private in many ways. We have our own very strong ideas. That type of person doesn't need a structured group or club or whatever. We're too individualistic for that.

Communitas in Xiamen was a performance of the value of individualism and the paradoxical quest for community and was celebrated here as a joint understanding of basic assumptions of Western society and the values that underpin global mobility. These commonalities in terms of shared value structures were only recognized through the stripping away of symbols of rank and structure of culturally bounded homelands. The common experience of such strangerhood allowed for a sense of 'togetherness' which was considered more equal and unbounded by the hierarchies of home:

> At home everyone knows where you went to school and what your father does for a living. Here, you could be anyone and it doesn't matter. Your friends don't know anything about what you do at home and you don't really care that much.
>
> (Female, 26, UK)

This liminal period was characterized by normlessness, spontaneity and an awareness of social bonds and a sense of equality. Perceived to be free of the structures of home and hierarchy, the Xiameners began to reconsider and reconstruct what it meant to be 'Western' and to belong to a particular nation and locality. Yet this journey led inevitably to the recreation of new identities and communities on a different ground between the local, the national and the global. This creative journey was possible because of the conflicting pulls and tensions between opposing experiences of structure and liminality, freedom and constraint, individualism and communalism and between familiarity and difference. The journey allowed for these tensions to be recognized and renegotiated and then reconstructed.

Rather than disappearing from purview the concepts of place, structure and emotion are central to the maintenance of the moral landscape of globalism. 'Rootlessness' and ambivalence can be seen as a part of a larger journey that is central to the continued relevance of thick forms of solidarity and place-based notions of identity and community.

Conclusion

Liminal Xiameners underwent a process of 'stepping outside themselves' – their location in cultural space was for now ambiguous and as such they experienced emotional extremes and behaved in ways that they felt they could not at other times and places – a phenomenon I have termed 'ecstasy'. However, being on the margins of social structure was experienced jointly with other liminal Xiameners. *Communitas* was a form of social interaction which is more spontaneous and less constricting with regard to norms and values. Stripped of signifiers of hierarchy and rank and with the knowledge that one doesn't need to 'play by the rules' of either the host or the home society, bonds were formed with others based on values that underpin globalism such as individualism and freedom. Narratives of breaking the rules, being free, equal and unstructured were common within interviews with Xiameners.

It was here, in this state of liminality and *communitas*, that what was previously considered common sense was brought into question. Many Xiameners underwent a process of social displacement and re-evaluation of what they had in common with other Westerners, their compatriots and with the Chinese. This questioning of self and structure was also a process of creativity. Aware of one's position on the margins of social structure, and liberated from place-based identity markers, they were able to recognize, reconsider and reconstruct notions of self, community and solidarity.

Being in temporal and cultural limbo for a period of time allowed those to whom I spoke to question the structures of home, to reconsider their relationships to others and to reflect and create new forms of identity, social structure and systems of rank. It was through negotiating the tensions between individualism and communalism, between freedom and constraint and between difference and familiarity that this process occurred.

With the weakening of relevance of social signifiers and stereotypes of home, the liminal Xiameners felt separated from society and, in their isolation, found themselves in a time of reflection (Aguilar 1999).

This liminal space resembled a 'laboratory...in which new ways of experimenting with ordering society are tried out' (Hetherington 1997: 12–13).

This liminal time of reflection and the later recreation of social structure revalidate and reconstitute notions of place, emotion and social structure as meaningful and connected categories of transnational sociality. Indeed, this mirrors the ideas of Park in 1928, long before the advent of concepts of postmodern identities, regarding the personal consequences of globalization. Park described the migrant as 'marginal man' who underwent a period of 'release from society' upon arrival in a new place. This 'emancipation' was eventually to be followed:

> ...in the course of time by the reintegration of the individuals into the social order. In the meantime, however, certain changes take place – at any rate are likely to take place – in the character of the individuals themselves. They become, in the process, not merely emancipated but enlightened.
>
> ([1928] 1969: 242)

Like Park's marginal men, many Xiameners would be reintegrated into a changed social order. This was only possible, however, because for this period of time 'he learns to look upon the world in which he was born and bred with something of the detachment of a stranger' (Park [1928] 1969: 242). This transformative journey was found within the narratives of many of those I interviewed and spoke with in Xiamen.

The applicability of the concepts of Turner (1969) and the social type described by Park ([1928] 1969) to this contemporary context suggests that global social research still needs to be located in historical as well as spatial contexts (Soja 1989). This reminds us also that while new types of migration are being outlined and indeed experienced, these remain continuations of historical processes of transnationalism and globalization. However, moving away from 'home' to a place of perceived difference allows for the creation of a localized context for the questioning of these historical power structures.

4
Fear and Difference

While the usual norms and rules of home were suspended, many Xiameners were in a position to reconsider their social identity and social position within a wider value context described here as the 'moral landscape' of globalization. The weakening of rules associated with the social structures of home led to the awareness of values that were associated with home and the ability to reconsider and replace one's self within this moral landscape.

Changes emerged in social relations at the global as well as the micro-level, made possible through the conditions of liminality. Appiah's (2006) notion of value 'conversations' can be used to explore how the values associated with globalism were reconsidered in a place of perceived difference. For Appiah (2006), cosmopolitan identity is a moral conversation about values across societies. He explains that he uses 'the word "conversation" not only for literal talk but also as a metaphor for engagement with the experience and the ideas of others' (Appiah 2006: 85).

Archer (2007) uses a similar notion of the 'internal conversation' to describe the process of mediation between social context and individual concerns and selfhood. Likewise, Taylor (1985) emphasizes human being's capacity for self-interpretation. For Taylor, this self-interpretation is not based on *a priori* epistemological principles but 'on practical knowledge and everyday encounters with cultural frameworks' (1985: 47). This notion of 'cultural frameworks' is, for Taylor, moral. He says, 'interpretation necessarily involves the evaluation of moral work' (1985: 48). I use the notion of the conversation to represent this process of reflexive interpretation which leads to the situating of selves within a moral landscape.

The experience of liminiality encouraged such 'conversations' to take place between discourses of globalism and localism, freedom and constraint, familiarity and difference, and individualism and the community. Arriving in Xiamen, the participants were faced with cultural and linguistic difference, and this distance began a conversation between discourses of the values of familiarity and difference. The conversation occurred within the context of what participants often described as a difficult and sometimes as a hostile environment.

I conceptualize the experience of chaotic place using the emotional structure of fear. This emotional structure is understood here as the social and personal expression of awareness of the non-existence of regular, 'normal' ways of thinking, acting and behaving and the subsequent interpretive action which results from this awareness. The emotional *structure* of fear therefore differs from its psychological equivalent. In analysing interview narratives, discourses of 'fear' as an affective state (such as fear of danger or poor hygiene) were just one indicator of the emotional structure of fear. Other indicators of this emotional structure included anger, frustration, patience and 'being lost' (see Figure 1). The emotional structure of fear was the way these various indicators – which all indicate a relationship to difference – led to the eventual interpretation and understanding of this perceived difference.

It was the process of interpreting, understanding and attempting to control this perceived difference that led to the eventual reconstruction of community bonds and what Appadurai (1996) referred to as 'neighbourhood' or meaningfully localized social groups. According to Appadurai (1996: 179), 'the production of a neighbourhood is inherently colonising in the sense that it involves the assertion of socially (and often ritually) organised power over places and settings that are viewed as potentially chaotic or rebellious'. The process of learning and understanding the local environment took place as identity and community were reconsidered and reconstructed. As the city itself became legible (Raban 1974), so did others, and this impacted on self-identity and the presentation of self. This chapter describes the process of making the city and the self 'legible'. It was the reactions to notions of difference and familiarity that formed the basis of the emergence of new subgroups and divisions in the local Xiamen community.

The experience of marginality – of being on the edge of social structure and familiarity – became central to the eventual reconstruction of social order. Social structure and division were constituted in relationship to the evolving moral landscape of home – that is, to the process of identifying, to differing degrees, with their own society as opposed to those which the Xiameners saw as the 'Other' (Van den Abbeele 1980: 11). This process can be seen as intricately linked to the recognition, reconsideration and reconstruction of the values that underpin global mobility.

Globalization is often posited as a process that pushes Western modernity to its extremes. The result, according to some postmodern theorists (such as Bauman, Beck and Turner), is a condition of rootlessness, ambivalence and a sense of uncertainty. For such theorists, the hyper-expression of the values which underpin global processes (such as the values addressed here – individualism, freedom and difference) contributes to the demise of solidarity and social cohesion. However, the centrality of the value placed on difference contributes to the continuation of notions of place, social structure and emotion in global lives. It was through the very processes of global mobility that community structure, emotional practice and place remained central facets of social lives and communal identities.

The emotional structure of fear is the basis upon which the renegotiation, or the conversation, of identity and belonging is founded. I use the emotional structure of fear to demonstrate how social action and identity were related to the way skilled transnational workers in Xiamen positioned themselves within a wider moral landscape. This 'positioning of self' formed the basis of a social hierarchy and the formation of a localized community in an environment that was distanced and different from the place and time known as 'home'. The reactions and responses to the emotional structures of anxiety, ecstasy and fear eventually result in newly reconsidered and reconstituted social bonds and divisions.

The emotional structure of fear

The experience of ecstatic liminality occurred as a result of an awareness of cultural difference upon arrival in Xiamen. This difference, however, was also experienced as the emotional structure of fear. When the rules and notions of common sense of home no longer seem to apply, it was not always certain how routines of everyday life will evolve. Many Xiameners hence also experienced a heightened sense of uncertainty. Linguistic barriers also led to a sense of powerlessness which contributed to this experience of vulnerability in day-to-day life.

Each of these emotional structures – anxiety, ecstasy and fear – relates to a wider experience of vulnerability. The tensions between central opposing facets of the moral landscape – individualism and the community, freedom and control and familiarity and difference – resulted in the vulnerable status of many Xiameners as they underwent a process of locating themselves between these opposing constructs. These Xiameners were vulnerable because they were in the process of defining themselves in relation to others and hence their status and their position within a moral landscape.

This vulnerability was constituted by the experience of the emotional structure of fear as Xiameners were faced with what they perceived as a dangerous and illegible urban environment. This application of the emotional structure of fear resonates with Bauman's (2006: 2) notion of fear as 'the name we give to our uncertainty: to our ignorance of the threat'. He equates fear to the sentiment of 'feeling insecurity and vulnerability' (2006: 3).

However, rather than this vulnerability necessarily contributing to a condition of heightened ambivalence and fluid uncertainty, it is part of a longer journey towards the legitimation and construction of social structure and relatively thick forms of solidarity. The experience of vulnerability also indicates the continued relevance of emotional interaction and interpretation for social change.

As Barbalet (1998: 147) pointed out, fear does not necessarily inhibit action. Fear directs change through an actor evaluating the risks and benefits of a particular course of action and what might be done to achieve them. It was differences in the perception of risks and the decision over courses of action as a result of vulnerability which were to form the basis of social hierarchy in Xiamen. The actor uses the experience of the emotional structure of fear to map the coordinates of power, place and community.

The analysis of the emotional structure of fear uncovers the way Xiameners begin to make sense of the world around them and either distance themselves from or attach themselves to the local environment. I use two examples of the emotional structure of fear that were indicated within interview discourse and fieldwork in Xiamen: perceptions of disorder and uncleanliness. By discussing these indicators of the emotional structure of fear, the participants were locating themselves as having a particular relationship not only with the local environment but with the values and expectations of their own taken-for-granted culture and ideas of what it means to be 'Western'.

Disorder

In the eyes of the interview participants, the traffic on Xiamen island was chaotic and lawless. While motorbikes were banned on the island itself, bicycles, cars, buses and pedestrians weaved what appeared to the

Westerner to be a suicidal web of disorder on the roads. The traffic was a constant topic of conversation among Xiamen's Western population and, rather than flippant chatter about the lack of road rules, it became evident that this fear of the traffic was a real and poignant daily experience for Xiameners. The perceived disorder on the roads was a visible, tangible and frightening manifestation of cultural difference that was negotiated by the participants on a day-to-day basis.

Jack, a 55-year-old English teacher from Canada, said:

> Some things frustrate me ... and you've probably heard about it from everyone – the traffic. Nothing so shocks me here. I've gotten used to all the little things, but the traffic is not a little thing. It's a big thing. On every given day, how many accidents do you see? There are so many! I think it's the lack of care for rules and regulation. A five thousand tonne machine coming down on you while you're driving a five thousand tonne machine – you are not aware of everything around you. It can kill you in a second. The main thing here that bothers me is the lack of care. The traffic is a huge part of life here. Even when you are walking on the sidewalk, your life is endangered by the traffic ... I think, don't you love your family and friends? If you do, why do you drive like that?

For Jack, the daily frustration he experienced in the urban environment led directly to a 'conversation' about morality and values. Through this encounter with the emotional structure of fear, Jack became aware that he values rules and regulations, and he views the lack of compliance in China as immoral – as a lack of love or concern for others.

Patrick was a business consultant originally from South Africa and educated in Australia. He had been in Xiamen for more than 10 years at the time of the interview. Nevertheless, he still continued to engage in this 'value conversation' using the traffic as his example:

> There is a guy standing in the middle of the road and everyone just goes around him. They don't let him walk past, they just go around him. This, I think, is a classic example. We have rules – between this line and this line is mine – you get in the way and I'm going to run you over. This is my life and I have the right to run you over because you are in my line.

Patrick became aware that in the West ideally there are rules for individual rights and obligations. He observed the lack of order on the

Xiamen roads and reflected upon his own position within a moral land-scape. At home, Patrick perceived that each individual person should have ownership of a particular space and the disorder he experienced in China was a manifestation of the breakdown in what he considered his rights as an individual. As a result of the emotional structure of fear, both Jack and Patrick began to reconsider notions of 'Western' values and the moral landscape of home. For many, the traffic in Xiamen epit-omized the disruption of what was previously thought of as 'common sense' or 'human values'.

This conversation (Appiah 2006) between specific and universal values was brought about through the experience of vulnerability. The following example from my field notes further highlights the relationship between the emotional structure of vulnerability and the reconsidering of notions of 'Western-ness' and the value of individualism:

There was a car accident last night. Dave was on his way home from the pub pretty early in the morning. On his way home he saw an accident had only just happened at a major intersection. A car was overturned. A crowd had gathered around the smoking car and he stopped and went to see what was happening. He saw there were two people in the car but no one in the crowd was doing anything to help. They were just watching. Waiting? Dave ran to the car and broke one of the doors and pulled the people out – a young man and a woman. They were badly injured. He called the police and the ambulance and got angry at the crowd. The police arrived and they questioned him. After the ambulance took the cou-ple away Dave was furious. He said he didn't understand why no one would help.

This morning he stopped past for a chat and he said 'don't they value each other? I always assumed helping other people was a human trait but even after this long in China I am still surprised by this group mentality. This group fear. They are all standing together watching. Not one single person is willing to put themselves out there. It took a foreigner to do it. Don't they feel shame about that?'

We spoke about the remnants of the Cultural Revolution and fear of the police and the communal nature of Chinese society, but he still said that he was so upset that his belief in individual people being courageous had been hung out to dry and he felt really disillusioned.

(Field diary entry, 25 October 2005)

This field-diary entry demonstrates how key themes of research often emerge from the fieldwork itself. Here, I interpreted Dave's response to the incident as a statement about the experience of difference, and I was later able to link it to the emotional structure of fear. I described how it was in response to difference and to what Dave perceived as a dangerous situation that the values of home came into discussion. Here, Dave was discussing his own location in a moral landscape. I do not suggest in this entry that Dave had experienced some kind of epiphany; rather, I indicate that the way he interpreted cultural difference was framed in discourse of values and morality, 'us' and 'them' and 'right and wrong', and that through my own experiences I reinterpreted the experience of others in a way that made sociological sense.

Leonard's (2010a) research into white identities in Hong Kong describes how the Chinese were imagined in the colonial imagination through a discourse of social disorder which positioned them as 'barbaric, criminal, rootless, and lawless' (p. 513). These images of 'evil and moral danger' (Leonard 2010a: 513) were, to an extent, alive and well within contemporary Western discourse in Xiamen, providing support to Leonard's theorizing that colonial discourse continues to weave its way through contemporary global mobilities (2010a: 530). The Othering of Chinese people as disorderly and immoral was constructed in Xiamen in relation to an idealized concept of the West which was seen as being threatened.

The emotional structure of fear in the face of perceived disorder was framed in terms of discourses on values. Rights, rules, obligations and the individual were all brought into focus through the daily experience of the traffic. The perceived difference led to the recognition of values inherent in specific social structures, in particular the values associated with 'home', and the subsequent repositioning of the self within a moral landscape.

The unclean

The emotional structure of fear was also indicated through discussions over hygiene. The disorder of difference was manifested in frequent discussions among the Western community about what was perceived to be uncleanliness in the urban environment. Idealized Western perceptions of hygiene and socially acceptable standards of behaviour were brought into question daily by Xiameners who saw themselves as vulnerable in this unclean physical and moral environment. This uncleanliness was often related to discussions about values and ideas of Western-ness. Gail, a 59-year-old English teacher from New York, said:

> I was looking at a student yesterday while he was doing an exam and he was just sitting there picking his nose. I thought, no! You're going to give me that paper too! They'll do it anywhere and I just hate that. All these things that irritate me are hygiene related. Once I was on a bus and I was standing and this woman had a child in her lap and she sort of nudged me and I looked down and she was letting her baby piss on the floor of the bus! I don't know enough Chinese, and I looked at her and she knew I was unhappy and I just said *bu hao* [bad] and moved away from her. I thought, it's a good thing the kid didn't have to shit!... and you see that on the streets all the time.

Such discussions about dirt, socially 'dirty' behaviour such as spitting or Gail's example of picking noses and urinating often served to form a conceptual moral boundary between 'us' and 'them'. What was perceived to be a standard of social cleanliness led to a continuing 'conversation' locating the Westerner in a moral landscape where the values and beliefs in Western ideals were justified and reinforced while simultaneously producing social boundaries between the Westerner and their Chinese 'Other' and the local environment. Tellingly, the presence of unclean, dangerous or disorderly places and conduct at home was rarely brought into this equation because this perceived urban difference was used to represent an idealized version of the morality home. This ideal moral landscape became equated to ideas of 'Western-ness'.

For example, the emotional structure of fear was described by Susan from England who reported on what she saw as a cultural difference in terms of cleanliness:

> The biggest shock of all of course was the dirt. I mean, these people who are so personally clean yet filthy. We find ourselves eating in restaurants that we would never eat in if this were back home. We would just not go in the door. But OK, I haven't gotten sick from it yet so... if you didn't want to eat at places like that you just wouldn't go to any restaurants here.

The emotional structure of fear, indicated here by discussion of the dirty or unclean, served to begin a process of considering what is different and familiar about 'here' and 'there' as well as 'us' and 'them'. Fechter (2007) also found that expatriates in Indonesia used the notion of 'The West' to symbolize 'civilization', order and purity 'while Indonesia stands for "non-civilization", disorder, and pollution in physical as well as symbolical terms' (p. 85). In Xiamen, this was also the case as the perceived threat of the unclean was linked to a moral discourse on Western-ness and the values which underpin globalism.

Such value conversations were also related to doing business in China, where the discourse often focused on how local practices challenge Western preconceptions of right and wrong. Nigel, 52, from the United Kingdom claimed that:

> Corruption I find everywhere. From the smallest level upwards. Staying out of that is a blessing. Because I am a foreigner I am able to stay out of that. But, quite truthfully, if I was Chinese I know it would be very difficult to stay out of it. I do find that a big downside as well.

Anderson's (1991) examination of the construction of Chinatown in Vancouver, Canada, also explored this relationship between the creation of place and moral boundaries. She found that as Chinese people began to gather around DuPont Street, this new 'Chinatown' began to be seen as a natural centre of vice, depravity, dirt, disease and immorality. The racial designation 'Chinese' was seen as synonymous with moral failure and was identified with a particular place – Chinatown. Anderson shows how Chinatown was not simply a natural reflection of Chinese culture but the result of a discourse constructed by those with the power to define place in order to reaffirm a moral order between 'us' and 'them'.

Anderson's study raises important issues about the power inherent in defining places as ideological sites of difference. The participants' creation of Xiamen as a place of difference should in no way be read as reflective of an essential, objective 'Chinese-ness'. Rather, its significance lay in the perceived difference between different environments, which led to the defining of Xiamen as the opposite to what was understood as familiar, right, 'normal' and reasonable. In other words, the imagining or defining of Xiamen as Other reaffirmed the ideal moral landscape of home.

The qualification needs to be made that the repositioning of the self and others within a moral landscape did not necessarily result in a negative perspective on the Chinese 'Other'. At times, the difference which was experienced through the emotional structure of fear led to an awareness of the boundaries between mutual expectations and standards. This awareness of one's own culture often led to a 'conversation' about the advantages of the 'Other' system and a rethinking of the validity of Western ideals. For example, Craig from the United States observed:

> That's what I love about China. You can have the man-hole off on the sidewalk. You walk down Zhong Shan Street and you see all this debris and everything everywhere. There could be a big man-hole and you could fall in it and break your leg. But there's no court here. It's your fault. You should have watched where you were going. I really like that about the Chinese versus our way ... In America there is too much red tape. In China it is the handshake. And they all, pretty much, will stay to their word as long as they're not being walked on. They still have the handshake type of agreement and you kind of start thinking, maybe there's something to that.

In this example, Craig expressed the cultural expectations of the West in terms of rights, legality and governance and through this framework reconsidered how he positioned himself in relation to such values and ideals. The next chapter shows how the process of resistance to what are perceived as Western concepts and values as well as their reacceptance helped form the basis of the social structure of the emerging community in Xiamen.

These reflexive 'conversations' between 'familiarity' and 'difference' led to an awareness of what were previously understood to be common ways of looking at the world and a reconsidering of where Xiameners placed themselves within a moral landscape. The emotional structure of fear is also implicated at the group level through the construction of notions of 'patience' and the management of emotional extremes.

Patience and emotional management

The emotional structure of fear not only led to a reconsideration of values and notions of common sense understandings of the world but also resulted in the emergence of discourses of 'coping' with and understanding perceived difference.

'Patience' was often spoken about by participants as an emotional tool that needed to be consciously practiced and performed in response to the unfamiliar urban environment. Anger and frustration at the perceived chaotic environment were found within the interviews as indicators of the emotional structure of fear and were linked to discourse on the need for the management of emotional extremes through patience.

Jess, a 21-year-old from England, explained the source of this anger and frustration when she reflected: 'I think it's one of those things that if you get told your apples are not apples, they're carrots you might get a bit pissed off.' The daily confrontations associated with the questioning of taken-for-grantedness led to frustration. Jack (52, Canada) noted how this questioning led to an awareness of the advantages of the emotional skill of patience:

> I admire them for not getting road rage. Why aren't you mad? Why aren't you mad at this person? As a passenger you get more angry and you think, man, you're calm through this! I'm getting heated! I want a gun! I am starting to accept it. It's like, yeah, ok. What can you do?

Jack's extreme emotional response to perceived disorder and danger led him towards an attitude of acceptance of the values of the 'Other'. Rather than acting immediately on his anger or frustration, he learnt to accept difference through patience.

Likewise, Melissa, a kitchen equipment trader from the United States, described how being faced with an unfamiliar environment helped reflect on larger structures and their relationship to the emotional management of the self:

> It comes in waves. It really does. You build up to a major level of frustration and then you realize you have to stop or you are going to suicide or kill people! You have to make a conscious effort and it doesn't happen overnight but after a month or so you start to chill out a bit. Because after a while you realize that you can't work at that level of frustration and continue to live here.

This development of awareness of difference and the emotional management to deal with it eventually formed the basis of divisions in the Western community in Xiamen as people became aware that not all Westerners cope with difference in the same way. Such divisions signalled the rise of a stratified, localized community while this research was being undertaken. While this is described in detail later, it is worthwhile prefacing it here with Melissa's reflections:

> There are some people, and they tend to be in the 40–50-year-old male western sector – they are so bitter and condescending and so judgmental and they don't make any effort to understand the

culture that they are living in or try to even rationalize the differences. You know, *why* does China not do things the way we do it? Well, because they've only been industrial for ten to fifteen years and they don't have the infrastructure. *Why* is the traffic so bad? Well, because its infrastructure, education ... They don't make the attempts to understand. They are really just here to make a buck and marry a Chinese woman who will take care of them the way their Western wives that they have divorced however many times didn't take care of them.

Melissa's analysis revealed the beginnings of divisions being created not just between the Westerner and the Chinese 'Other' but between Westerners based on their reactions to difference and their position within a moral landscape. Melissa's reflections pointed to the construction of both gendered and radicalized differentiations, which will be discussed in detail later. Here, it is relevant to note that it was in relation to contrasting perceptions of difference that this social redivision took place.

Bill was a 58-year-old Australian and was a retired employee of a major multinational company that had a regional facility based in Xiamen. He now taught English at the university. He discussed these divisions within the Western community in terms of 'being on guard' in social interactions:

> It doesn't matter how long you've been here, you'll always think, why did you do that? Why did you say that? About the Chinese. We just can't understand why they do some things. I get frustrated. Sometimes I get angry. They tend to yell and scream a lot but I don't know if it's because they are really angry or because it's just their culture.

> I suppose our culture and customs are ingrained in us so it's not easy to understand it. Well, we can understand but after a while it gets wearing on you ...

> I find one of the biggest problems in my mind is that you are on your guard all the time. Am I going to make a fool of myself? Am I going to say the wrong thing? Am I going to upset someone? You are continuously on your guard and that becomes very tiring.

> So when you go back to Australia you are not on your guard. You know how to approach someone, you know what to do but here you don't. You have to think about your behaviour here.

> Some Westerners here don't care. They just say what they want and they don't care if they offend. Some foreigners behave differently here than they would at home.

Here Bill separated himself from the 'other' Westerners who don't interact with 'consideration' and conscious thought about applicable social behaviour. He attempted to justify the differences he faced by saying that his 'customs are ingrained in him' and through admitting that he doesn't always understand the differences he faces. Bill linked this awareness of difference ('We just can't understand why they do some things') with indicators of the emotional structure of fear ('I get angry', 'You are on your guard all the time') and with the ecstatic liminality described previously ('Some foreigners behave differently here than they would at home'). As these Xiameners became aware of being on the margins of social regulation of home, the awareness of difference was heightened. It was in the various means of interpreting difference that the values that underpin global mobility and the thick social structure of home began to be reconsidered.

The awareness of local social structures and culturally inscribed norms and expectations led some Westerners in Xiamen to engage in a form of value conversation with other Westerners. The emotional structure of fear resulted in a discourse of difference and attempts to interpret the local environment at the group level.

Communal patience and development discourse

The way Xiameners considered the cultural difference and the chaotic urban environment they faced demanded a means of coping with, or negotiating, the disorder they observed. As we have seen, one means of interpreting or 'making legible' the environment was for the Westerner to develop emotional skills such as patience. This production of patience at the individual level is also performed in a group setting through the production of specific language and myths used to understand what was seen as an unfamiliar environment. The existence of such stories passed on through networks indicated the emergence of a local and contextually based community and solidarity among Westerners in Xiamen.

The first of these locally produced language codes to be addressed here was popularly known in Xiamen as T.I.C., or 'This is China'. Josie, a 26-year-old English teacher from Australia, explained the colloquialism:

> When something gets so frustrating, or so unexplainable that you just can't see any answers for it at all then you say 'TIC'. This is China. It just means that you shouldn't look for reasons why they do things

different. It's just different. It's not a bad thing. It just means that it's not better or worse here – it's just different. Full stop. Stop stressing out about it and just accept it.

'T.I.C.' was recounted in some locations around Xiamen but not all. This particular phrase was used only in some places by some people. It was an indication of the emergence of a subgroup in Xiamen, and in this case such a colloquialism was used by those who sought a degree of difference and who were in Xiamen as short- to medium-term teachers or travellers. Similar phrases, however, were used by others outside this subgroup:

> There is a little Western joke – you are describing something to a Westerner, and then it comes down to assigning a cause, they say 'the Chinese are the Chinese'. If you can't go to the point of explanation, all you can say is that they are Chinese. It's just the way they do it. You can't explain it.
>
> (Male, 52, England)

This shared language indicated the beginnings of subgroup formation based on length of time spent in the country and knowledge of place. The emergence of such shared phrases was a means to understand or accept cultural difference at a group level.

The second example of a communal attempt to interpret urban difference was shared by a diverse selection of participants with different lengths of stay in China, occupations and nationalities. When faced with the perceived indecipherable environment, the Westerners located this difference within a larger temporal framework that they were familiar with. They explained the perceived chaos and difference by relating the development of China to the time frame of Western history. These stories all appealed to a common understanding that China is 'catching up' on the linear time frame of development paved by Western countries. For example, Stephanie from Denmark offered the following explanation for difference:

> After long-term exposure to those small differences you get really frustrated, and you know China doesn't have infrastructure or the experience that we have as an industrialised nation. They're still building up that infrastructure.

By positioning China along a linear development path whereby it ultimately will result in being more 'understandable' or legible through its progressive modernization, some Westerners were able to place their experience of the emotional structure of fear in a larger structural context that 'makes sense' to them, relative to their experiences of home.

Such linear time frames of progressive development can be related to mainstream modernist perspectives of development and progress, particularly those influenced by Parsons (1966) and Rostow ([1960] 1990) who perceived the Third World as progressing along a linear path paved by the West towards a more advanced and sophisticated stage known as modernity. This is not to say that China hasn't also followed linear development models (most notably, of course, Marxist and Maoist models). What is relevant here is the *perception* by Westerners that the stage of development along a linear path to modernity was what differentiated 'us' from 'them' and was used to make sense of, or make legible, that which was considered different. This discourse also served to reinforce or legitimate the very processes of progress and modernity that constituted the moral landscape of home.

This process of rationalizing difference along Western development standards was also discussed in terms of the values of the Chinese, which were perceived by some to be at a position the West 'was' before it reached a higher state of development. For example:

> I see rich people over here and they have no concept. A lot of them, they just want to wear a watch because it's expensive. They want to drive a car just to be seen. We don't do it at home to quite the same degree... Obviously, a lot of the patterns that are occurring here due to the wealth have already happened back home in the West. The yuppie in the 80s, you know, it's the same kind of thing that is going on... We've kinda been through that and it's finished, you know, it's gone.
>
> (Male, 30, UK)

Modern values such as progress and linear development framed the reactions to difference and provided a means to both reassert and reconsider these value structures. Home was idealized as a place that existed at a higher stage of 'progress' than Xiamen. Different periods of Western developmental history were used to understand cultural difference. Here, Bill (58, Australia) equated the Chinese to his own generation:

> Sometimes I equate this younger generation of the Chinese to my generation when I was growing up. Because their parents were

involved in the Cultural Revolution and they had a pretty rough time even though some of them are now quite wealthy. I tend to think of that in terms of my experience of Depression and World War II parents. Our parents when they were growing up were probably fairly poor but our generation is quite wealthy or had good jobs and now have inherited their parent's wealth. I kind of equate a similarity.

Bill was able to comprehend the difference he experienced by placing it in a realm of understanding that he is familiar with. Such stories, which make difference legible by placing it in a context of wider global and Western concepts of time and place, became the foundations of a sense of community in Xiamen. Such common language and common symbols and values were facilitated through the emotional structure of fear.

Farrer (2010) also recounts the manipulation of concepts of place and time by long-term Western settlers in Shanghai. He describes how narratives of expatriate emplacement were not reduced to a single postcolonial temporality. Rather, long-term expatriates situated themselves within multiple temporalities – described as being either postcolonial, post-socialist or postmodern. Farrer suggests that by shifting between these time-lines, the Shanghai expatriates attempted to 'achieve an attachment to a rapidly changing place by playing with modalities of time' (2010: 1226). The Xiameners played with modalities of time by using linear developmental temporality to explain – and make sense of – perceived difference.

Concepts of time and place were used as a means of interpreting what is seen as a chaotic or rebellious urban environment. Time and place were used as conceptual markers around which social actors comprehended their role in global mobility and made links between their own action and the wider social structures and processes in which this action was embedded. In other words, time and place were used as a defining mechanism.

The process of defining difference was a process of attributing meaning and value to what was previously an illegible cultural environment. This illegibility was experienced through the emotional structure of fear which was indicated within interviews by various reactions to difference, including anger, frustration, fear and patience. This emotional structure of fear led to the development of mechanisms to make the environment 'legible' and hence less potentially threatening or chaotic. Emotional skills such as patience were consciously developed in order to counteract the vulnerability felt in day-to-day life and a common language of understanding difference began to develop among many

Westerners in order to make sense of the world around them. This common understanding and common experience of defining the city and the concurrent repositioning of the self within a moral landscape were to become the basis of a more structured community in Xiamen. It is through knowledge, or understanding, of difference that social boundaries within the Western population began to form.

Conclusion

The period of liminality following arrival was a necessary precursor to the development of a contextualized community in Xiamen. The perceived freedom from the structures of home allowed for a period of awareness of the values and rules of 'home'. This heightened awareness of cultural, linguistic and urban difference was experienced through the emotional structure of fear as the taken-for-granted effects of behaviour no longer seemed to apply. The interpretation of difference led to a reconsideration of values and a questioning of common sense means of thinking that were now considered to be 'Western'. The interpretation of difference sometimes led to the conscious development of emotional skills such as patience. In its communal form, this translated into shared discourse which served to 'make legible' the perceived chaotic environment.

The ability to make the environment legible was a form of power held by those who had been in China the longest, and who had the greatest knowledge of the place and how to negotiate cultural and urban differences. The power to define the city eventually became the basis for a reconstituted system of status and prestige.

After a period of being on the perceived margins of social structure, the beginnings of forms of sociality are renegotiated. This renegotiation was conducted as an ongoing 'conversation' between the local and the global. Vulnerability led to an internal and interactive discussion about the perceived values of an idealized notion of the 'West'. The ensuing conversation about difference and familiarity led to a rethinking of key values that underpin globalism.

In this way, we can see that global mobility and experience are related to a reaffirmation of the moral landscape and the values of individualism, freedom and difference. Claims that globalism is causing the concurrent demise of social cohesion and the relevance of place and emotion tell only one part of a larger story. The journey that is mapped here reveals an evolving yet continued relationship between place, structure and emotion for those who are globally mobile.

Anxiety, ecstasy and fear result in a dialogue between the ideologies of individualism and the community, between freedom and constraint and between familiarity and difference. These value 'conversations' (Appiah 2006) can also be expressed as a positioning of the self and others within a moral landscape. This renegotiation of the moral landscape often led to the creation of an idealized notion of the 'West' and the reaffirmation (or reconsideration) of values and systems of belief that the idea of the 'West' is perceived to represent. The result of these personal and social dialogues is often the production of new social divisions and solidarities.

These contemporary global mobilities are journeys away from the territoriality of home and lead to a time of structural liminality. Yet the place of home and the social structures it entails remain relevant to the lives of transnational Westerners *because* they are away. Further, rather than global mobilities resulting in a condition of ambivalent postmodern emotionlessness, forms of emotional action and practice remain central to the maintenance and continuation of the values that underpin globalism.

Part II describes the divisions and connections in Xiamen that are formed as a result of the journeys that have been recounted here. In this way we are tracing the journeys that continue to create the conditions for the construction and creation of place, emotion and social structure and the moral landscape of home.

Part II
Power and Community

5
Division

Each of the emotional structures explored here – anxiety, ecstasy and fear – is 'vulnerable', in the sense that they indicated a changing relationship with social structures where the participant's position within a moral landscape was in the process of being redefined. Three key values which underpin global mobility have been examined in relation to these emotional structures in order to understand the way that local experience interacts with wider global processes. These values are individualism, freedom and difference.

The emotional structure of anxiety was linked to the value of individualism which was experienced in opposition to the perceived demands and expectations of the community. Upon arrival in Xiamen, the participant experienced a perceived freedom from the expectations and norms of home. The Xiamener felt distanced from the rules and boundaries of both home and the local environment. This perceived weakening of structure was experienced by the participants through the emotional structure of ecstasy.

This liminality also meant that the Xiameners were faced with what was perceived as an illegible urban and cultural environment marked by uncertainty. This uncertainty was described as experienced through the emotional structure of fear. In order to understand or make legible the urban environment, the participants were involved in a negotiation between the opposing concepts of cultural familiarity and difference. These 'conversations' (Appiah 2006) between individualism and community, freedom and constraint, and familiarity and difference resulted in the reconsideration of the participant's location within a moral landscape.

Part II describes how these conversations formed the basis of the development of divisions and structures within the transnational population in Xiamen. The commonalities in the experience of what Turner (1969) called 'liminality' and what Park ([1928] 1969) termed 'release' are contrasted with the social divisions that began to form at the local level as a result of different responses to the experience of vulnerability. Here we follow the participants' re-engagement with community following the time of perceived weakening of social structure.

I am not claiming that community is objectively absent at any time among Westerners in Xiamen and is rebuilt following the liminal period. Rather, the experience of vulnerability and the weakening of social structure facilitate the conditions for individuals' re-engagement with community. It is relevant here to emphasize that the temporal ordering of this book from arrival through to the experiences of vulnerability upon arrival and *then* community is a means of conceptually pulling apart multiple and converging journeys from home. Not all participants were undergoing this time of liminality at the same time, nor was there a determined point of re-engagement with community and structure. Instead, the constant influx of new arrivals and the experiences of vulnerability helped shape a dynamic localized community in Xiamen. This dynamism indicates that structure and community continue to exist for those living outside their homelands yet are fashioned according to the experience of mobility.

This re-engagement with community in Xiamen was bounded by disciplinary mechanisms such as status, gender and race and nationality. In other words, re-engagement with community occurs *as* the participants reposition themselves within a moral landscape. In this way, the vulnerability that many postmodern theorists associate with notions of 'rootless' and ambivalent cosmopolitanism (Bauman 2007; Beck 2000) exists as part of a more complex and contextualized journey which continues to be bounded by notions of place, structure and emotional action.

This chapter describes the presence of community as indicated by the existence of a local status system. This social hierarchy was based on differing social reactions to experiences of vulnerability. Authority was constructed in Xiamen by those who found ways to control this sense of vulnerability at the local level and hence had the capacity to influence others' interpretation of the environment.

Status in Xiamen was renegotiated according to each participant's knowledge of place and the length of time they had spent in China. This capacity to define place became the basis of a social hierarchy. Divisions were subsequently formed not only between Westerners and the Chinese 'Other' but also *between* Westerners who positioned themselves differently within a moral landscape. Such divisions revealed the presence of subgroups in the city. The regulatory mechanisms of gossip and rumour were employed to maintain and reinforce the renewed sense of social structure. Local use of symbolic familiarity and difference indicated group membership and divisions. First, we explore the reconstruction of status and prestige associated with knowledge of place and time.

Old-timers and newcomers

Arriving in Xiamen for the first time, James checks into his room at the Crowne Plaza and, with the help of concierge, finds his way to a restaurant and bar frequented by Westerners. He orders a beer and strikes up a conversation with a group of young Americans and Australians at the next table. Rather than asking him where he is from or what he does for a living, the first question he is asked is 'how long have you been here?' When James replies 'about two hours' there are knowing nods around the table and sympathetic smiles. They ask James to join them and for the next three hours James is told stories of the 'real' China, how to get by, how to talk to taxi drivers, where to buy the best groceries, what to watch out for and be careful of. He notes that the person doing most of the talking is Roger, who has been in China for the longest amount of time, who speaks Chinese and who knows the contacts, factories and places that he says James should know about.

The hierarchy in this small gathering was based around the length of time spent in China and the knowledge of the place that could be passed on to others. Knowledge as a basis for hierarchy and division in an emerging community was spoken about by Michael from the United Kingdom:

> I know people that have been here for years – can't string a sentence together, don't know anything about Chinese culture or Chinese history or Chinese society. They know nothing. Then again, there are people who have lived in China a lot longer than I have and who know a lot more than I do.

In this quote, Michael was positioning himself along a hierarchy associated with knowledge of China and the length of time spent there. Within this hierarchy, a certain level of naivety was assumed on behalf of the newcomer by those who had been in China for a longer time. This 'naivety' placed those with more experience in a position of authority to shape the definition of place for those who were new arrivals. Transfer of knowledge, telling stories of dealing with vulnerability and offering advice were ways of asserting a more authoritative position within the community hierarchy.

This vulnerability, as we have seen, was characterized by the interpretation of an unfamiliar illegible urban environment. Knowledge about the city (such as where to go, how to get there and how to communicate) was seen as a means to understand or 'make legible' the urban environment. Those who developed the experience of place were also those who claimed to possess the necessary skills to 'deal with' (male, 34, England) or 'cope with' (female, 26, US) what was perceived as a sometimes hostile environment. Those with this interpretive knowledge hence held authority within a community hierarchy. Such authority was gained through length of time spent in China and previous experiences of vulnerability.

Such discourse on China as something to be 'dealt with' or 'battled against' is reflected in the growing genre of 'how-to' books which are marketed at those doing business in China. For example, Western businesses aiming to engage with the emerging industry sector in China can select from texts with titles such as *Taming the Dragon* (Jaeger 1994), *Managing the Dragon* (Perkowski 2008), *Lessons from the Frontlines of Doing Business in China* (MacGregor 2005) or Brahm's (2004) *Doing Business in China the Sun Tzu Way* which recounts 'war stories' and 'tactics' learned through experience 'in the field'. The authority of such texts rests on the Western authors' ability to have 'tamed' or 'managed' what is perceived as an illegible business environment likened to a 'war zone' or a 'frontier'. Their advice tends to follow the mantra that 'anyone who thinks the China road will be an easy one should stay away' (Perkowski 2008: 14).

From this perspective, China is not for the faint-hearted and those who have succeeded over the long term have earned authority through their 'stoicism' and self-determination in encountering the different environment. The accumulation of knowledge during this journey is sold in the form of advice books for those 'daring enough' to follow suit. This discourse also existed at the local level in Xiamen – those who had been through a journey of hardship in China had acquired knowledge which held authority within the local community.

Fechter's (2007) study of expatriates in Indonesia describes a 'hardship ideology' which was associated with her participants' lives. One element of this is the concept of expatriation as a state of deprivation, including the idea of the 'hardship post' (Fechter 2007: 3). The provision of additional benefits to compensate for a deprivation of perceived comfort and familiarity while posted is no longer common in China and few of those I spoke to in Xiamen were on such a package. However, this notion of expatriation as deprivation and hardship was still present and was associated with an individualistic sense of achievement.

Stories of 'doing it rough' in China and having succeeded through spending a prolonged period of time in the country or developing successful skills for doing business in China were common:

> I think those of us who came here back in that era [mid-1990s] are different from those here now. So many of the expats that are here today are here for different reasons…those of us in the early days came out of curiosity. But certainly, in 95, one had to be an absolute idiot to come to China as a teacher and to think you were going to make money. It was extremely poorly paid…but there were no luxuries then. No bars and no DVDs so what do you spend your money on anyway!
>
> (Male, 58, Australia)

This discourse on 'roughing it' was associated with a time of liminality and used as a contemporary metaphor of living in the 'wilderness' (Iyer 2001). This time without the perceived comforts of home also became a form of human capital (Schultz 1963) which contributed to the development of a status system within the Western community.

It was considered among old-timers in Xiamen that a certain degree of direct contact with cultural difference and vulnerability 'earned the right' to 'indulge' in the familiarity of home. Simon from the United Kingdom explained this:

> I find myself in increasingly cosmopolitan places. It surprises me, to be frank. I now have a pretty good job, live in a very nice apartment which is very Western-style. I have an Australian girlfriend, a group of friends which are predominantly foreigners. I find myself speaking English 95% of the time. I watch Western movies and read English books. I eat Western food. Which is completely counterpoint to where I was when I first arrived in China when I was more engrossed in China and Chinese-ness. I think, perhaps, I've *earned* a degree of cosmopolitanism.

Simon considered himself worthy of indulgence in consuming 'Westernness' because he had been through a period of being away from this familiarity. The consumption of familiarity and difference is discussed in detail later. Here, however, it is important to note that time spent in an unfamiliar place was considered by some to be a rite-of-passage or a ritual which could earn higher status within Xiamen itself. Newcomers were perceived by those such as Simon as yet to undergo a period of heightened vulnerability and, as such, were considered yet to have high status within this hierarchy.

Newcomers were yet to negotiate their position within their moral landscape. As recent arrivals, their identity and their sense of belonging in the local environment were yet to be defined. For the moment, their status remained ambiguous according to those who had established themselves within the local community.

The constant influx of new arrivals in Xiamen shaped the social hierarchy within the community. Without new arrivals onto whom knowledge of China and Xiamen and skills for getting by in an unfamiliar environment could be passed, the old-timers would not be able to continue to maintain their position of authority. As new arrivals underwent the process of making legible the unfamiliar environment in interaction with the old-timers, they too developed the knowledge and time spent in the city in order to position themselves higher within this status structure. In this way, the vulnerabilities of global mobilities are intricately linked to the reconstruction of social structure. This link between vulnerability and the re-engagement with social structure is evidenced by the emergence of hierarchies between 'newcomers' and 'old-timers' in Xiamen.

The flow of people in and out of the city was vital to the maintenance and production of division and hierarchy within Xiamen. The hierarchical relationship between old-timers and new-comers was most evident in the example of Carl. Carl sat at the top of the time/place knowledge hierarchy in Xiamen. He was well known in Xiamen and his rags-to-riches story held almost mythological status in the city's expatriate circles. Carl arrived in Xiamen in the late 1980s and struggled with corrupt business partners, the collapse of his business and an ensuing period of relative poverty. Carl continued to stay in Xiamen; he 'pursued and persisted against the Chinese' (male, 56, US) and was to build up the most successful foreign business start-up in the city, eventually becoming a multi-millionaire. Carl's story was one of making legible the unfamiliar environment and becoming successful as a result. While Carl's prestige was based on financial success, his status was maintained through his knowledge of the city and the time he had spent in China. While many talked about him with respect for his rags-to-riches tale, some also separated themselves from him at a moral level:

> He [Carl] likes to push his power around and treat people badly…He is just totally bizarre sometimes when we are out for dinner. I mean, I like the guy and everything but…of course he has 3000 employees so I guess he feels he can do that. He thinks he's a king. But he can be kind of disrespectful of the Chinese sometimes.
>
> (Male – details withheld)

This interviewee recognized that Carl held high authority in the community ('he likes to push his power') yet was keen to express that Carl was not similar to him in the way he viewed the Chinese environment and people ('he can be kind of disrespectful of the Chinese'). While status was linked to time spent in China and knowledge of place, division was also occurring according to the positioning of self within a moral landscape.

The status hierarchy in Xiamen served to separate Westerners from each other as they continued what Appiah (2006) called a 'conversation' about values and moral boundaries. The example of Carl demonstrates the construction of a system of status in the city alongside the awareness that other Westerners might not necessarily position themselves within the moral landscape in the same way. The 'conversation' that takes place concerns what I have described as key values that underpin global mobility: individualism and community; freedom and constraint; familiarity and difference. The positioning of the self with regard to these values has been described as the 'moral landscape'. Here, the example of Carl demonstrates that this positioning coincides with the re-engagement with hierarchy, status and community at the local level.

The presence of a system of hierarchy indicated the existence of a localized community in Xiamen. According to Scheff (1994: 8):

> In a society where most bonds are intact, money, power and sex and other such externals may appear to be motives in themselves, but they also symbolize a hidden motive, the maintenance or enhancement of one's standing in the eyes of others.

In Xiamen, the motives for staying in China and for developing the skills to 'cope with' difference also symbolized this same hidden motive: to enhance the Xiamener's image in the eyes of others. A Scottish engineer who had been in Xiamen for three years said:

> There are a lot of people who think they are more powerful than others on the social scene here. But they aren't really. There are others who try to trade on the perceptions of other people.

This interviewee was indicating not only that a status system existed in Xiamen but that status was able to be manipulated by those who understood its dynamics. This capacity for manipulation of authority suggests the presence of a community with accepted meanings and shared understandings of loyalties and priorities. The ability to 'trade on the perceptions of other people' was an indication of this shared value system and the presence of localised social structure. Status and prestige were being built on the ability to 'deal with' vulnerability. In the example of Carl, his authority rested on the length of time he had spent in China, his having been through a period of 'roughing it' and succeeding 'despite' the difficulties of an unfamiliar environment.

Such relationships between vulnerability and social structure suggest that the significance of the notions of postmodern 'rootlessness' lies not as a final condition or consequence of increased global mobility. Rather, such experiences of 'rootlessness' perform a valuable role in providing the necessary conditions for the recognition, reconsideration and reconstruction of place-bound forms of social structure.

Gossip and rumour

At the same time that Westerners in Xiamen were involved in a process of reconsidering the structures and value systems of home, they became aware of an explicit regulatory gaze in their new location. Gossip was rife within the Western community and served as a mechanism for regulating behaviour which fell outside the norms and standards deemed acceptable according to renegotiated notions of 'Western-ness'. The ecstatic behaviour which has been described as 'outside the boundaries of social structure' was reigned in through the presence of and potential for gossip and rumour within the Western community. As new arrivals began to reattach themselves to community, gossip and rumour began to function for them as latent reminders of the social 'rules' of home and community.

The regulatory and controlling power of gossip and rumour became more evident as the city itself began to develop a Western centre with regular spaces (restaurants, bars, parks) for differing subgroups within the foreign community. It was the gossip within these places in the city that can be seen as an example of community self-regulation. Xiameners began to be aware of the gaze of other Westerners and gossip networks that were both locally and globally meaningful. Callum explained the role of gossip in Xiamen:

Everybody here thinks that they can get away with everything and anything and it doesn't matter. But it does in the end. Because you can only buckle with someone so many times before the entire group knows about it and is wary. They'll be ok to you socially on that shallow level, but if you try to do anything else they won't touch you. Because of the way Xiamen is, because people come and go, there are a lot of guys that I know that come over from the States and the UK, they come over here regularly on business. It is becoming like a global network and if you make an arsehole of yourself to everyone that's here, then, every one of us has got friends, contacts, business relations or whatever in different countries... So not only have you made an arse of yourself to me, but you've made an arse of yourself to those guys. Because they'll ask me. And I'll tell them you're an idiot.

Callum's account indicates how gossip functioned as a form of a regulatory 'gaze' of home. He described ecstatic behaviour ('Everybody here thinks that they can get away with everything and anything and it doesn't matter') but says that eventually this behaviour will have repercussions both in Xiamen and in other places ('Its becoming like a global network'). As a sense of belonging developed in Xiamen ('the entire *group* knows about it') the rules of behaviour of 'home' began to again reassert themselves in a new context ('I'll tell them you're an idiot').

While Callum's quote emphasized that local gossip could result in *global* effects, such networks could also have *local* consequences. An excerpt from my field diary recounts this:

While the job market at this level is international – Hugo was dealing with transnational corporations, international head-hunters and was making trips back to France to find a job in China – it was the relationships that he had with people at locally in Xiamen that eventually got him his job... While global networks are expanding and business is being done by email and late night phone calls across multiple time-zones, the friend at the local coffee shop in Xiamen and your local reputation can often be where it counts. Your reputation with the person next to you is not losing its relevancy.

(Field diary entry, 26 September 2005)

Hugo lived what he considered a global lifestyle, yet when he was seeking a job change it was the local relationships and his reputation (as governed by systems of gossip) which resulted in his successful career move. Gossip provided evidence for the continuing significance of local relationships for those engaged with global careers.

Likewise, gossip was evidence of community as it sets the norms of membership in a group in diffuse ways that are beyond the control of private individuals. Gossip is always about particular people, related to particular people (Warner 2002: 59). Gossip, in this way, is a dividing practice which enables the production of status as a relationship which both constructs – and is constructed by – individuals. What you can get away with saying depends very much on whom you are speaking to and what your status is in that person's eyes. 'The right to gossip about certain people', writes Max Gluckman (1963: 313), 'is a privilege extended to a person when he or she is accepted as a member of a group or set. It is a hallmark of membership'. Gossip, therefore, was a signifier not only of the renegotiation of social values and norms but also of the membership status within defined social groups. Gossip is relevant here in an analysis of the social boundaries around which a transnational community is constructed because gossip is *never* a relationship among strangers (Warner 2002: 59). Gossip necessarily involves shared meanings, values and divisions.

As well as indicating the presence of community, gossip also indicated that this community was divided. This community and its division were connected to both the local Xiamen context and to forms of social structure at 'home'. In this instance, gossip was a means of re-engaging with these forms of social structure which were conceptualized as located at once 'elsewhere' and 'here'. We have seen how the meaning of the initial decision to leave home supported Jameson's (1988) claim that the meanings of action 'no longer coincide with the place in which they take place'. The repercussions of behaviour defined as deviant within gossip networks in Xiamen were linked to a notion of a place that was 'elsewhere' – home.

The regulatory role of gossip indicates re-engagement with social structure and community. Models of cosmopolitanism which argue that global mobility results in a condition of 'free-floating rootlessness' and the demise of 'place' tend to ignore the continued structural relevance of place, regardless of physical connectedness with territoriality. Global mobility does result in the experience of vulnerability; however this vulnerability provides the conditions for the reconstruction of place-centred notions of power, structure and community. The vulnerable processes described in Part I were 'reigned in' by mechanisms such as gossip which were seen to hold their relevance both at 'home' and within the Western community in Xiamen. Further, and importantly, gossip was also a means of creating, maintaining and reinforcing the system of status and hierarchy. Likewise, the exchanging of secrets was another means of maintaining relationships of trust and belonging.

Secrets and trust

Telling others something in confidence, whether this information was considered gossip or a secret, also indicated the presence of a form of social capital, such as trust. Confiding in another person initiated a connection with that person and an awareness of that person's connections with others in the local environment. Secrets were a vehicle for relationships of trust. Bonds and connections formed between people were based on the sharing of knowledge which others might not have had.

Business secrets were frequently swapped between Xiameners. Entrepreneurial traders often considered other Westerners as business competitors as well as friends. The relationship between business and friendship was not always clear for those who sought not only to understand the illegible urban environment but also to profit from this understanding. One respondent stated: 'It's true that the line between business and friendship is sometimes not clear in Xiamen' (male, 27, France). The capacity to know how to do business in China, how to get access to factories, business partners and staff, could directly impact on the success of an entrepreneurial trader. This information was often swapped in confidence or was given to other Westerners as a form of social gift. An excerpt from my field diary discusses the role of secrets and trust in maintaining bonds and creating divisions within the community:

> It still strikes me, this level of secrecy within the Western community in Xiamen. [A] works for [B], the head of an [international accessories company]. [C] is good friends with [D], a ladies accessories competitor from Sweden, but he is also good friends with [A] and [B]. So he has to watch what he says around them. There is a level of information they can all divulge, but the rest is closed for conversation. They are friends, and competitors... Secrets are a common currency here – 'this stays between us...' or 'I trust you not to tell anyone this...' are common phrases heard between friends. When my contacts start negotiations with a new job, they do not tell anybody the details and declare that it is very important that it is kept secret until the right time. It is hard to know why their negotiations must be kept secret but it is an interesting thought that this secrecy might induce a closer relationship, a feeling of importance and uniqueness. Who knows the secret and who shouldn't be told are important links in friendship chains and power plays. Secrets hold the dynamics of the

city – its emerging groups and its potential – and leaking secrets to others – a form of gossip of sorts – is important in confirming or reaffirming friendship.

(Field diary, 26 June 2005)

It became clear that secrets were an important marker of both community and shared understandings in Xiamen. As with gossip, secrets were swapped between people who knew where they stood in relation to others. My observation and interviews found this resulted in the construction and strengthening of social bonds, as well as the maintenance of divisions with those who did not have access to such information.

A side effect of this selective sharing of knowledge was a sense of being wary of relationships which may have been a disguise for gaining information. Callum said:

> With foreigners, there's always the thought that we probably come from similar backgrounds so you can probably trust them. But it turns out you've got to be wary of what you say. Everybody here talks about business when they are out. To be honest, that's the main reason why most people are here. Like, the ones who come here to seek their fortune because China is like the next big thing. People are trying to seek their fortunes and that's why they're here. Everybody is trying to get a piece of it. And unfortunately everybody is trying to get the same piece in the same way. It's like a race to the bottom and it's like, I've got to get my piece before everybody else gets theirs... It's seems like even when there is friendship being extended you are not sure if there are strings attached to it. Is that person just trying to be nice because they think you may be of value for something else that is going to come up in the future? You can see that there is always a lot of jockeying for position. There's always an awful lot of politics going on here.

Likewise, Carol reflected:

> I think I've become a lot more cynical. People always want something from you. I feel like it's difficult to meet people who just want to be nice, who just want to extend help or a hand for the sake of it. Just for the sake of being nice.

In these examples, Callum and Carol were discussing knowledge of the local environment and its relationship to business success.

This knowledge existed as a type of currency used for social exchange in Xiamen. Those who had the knowledge (whether cultural information, contacts, business know-how) held a position of authority because they could pass this information on to others at their discretion. This passing of knowledge formed part of the hierarchical system in Xiamen. Trusting others with information was precarious when such knowledge could be used to the benefit of competition. One result was that friendship and business became intertwined.

Dependency and co-dependency

The re-engagement with community bound by the regulatory mechanisms of gossip and trust was often based on the exchange of place-based forms of knowledge. The information that was exchanged in order to produce this sense of 'togetherness' and status division facilitated friendships which were considered by those in Xiamen as either dependent or co-dependent. In order to make sense of the city or to 'make it legible', the information held by others had to be seen as needed by those who lacked it.

Dependent relationships with others were more relevant for those who considered themselves in China as an 'individual' rather than as a part of a familiar corporate structure associated with 'home'. The formation of dependent relationships was a means to rectify the experiences of vulnerability which were a part of being 'outside' the structures and norms of home.

Marion's (42, Australia) experience highlights the links between individualism, vulnerability and dependent relationships. Marion arrived in Xiamen ten years ago on a contract with a large multi-national company. During her years with the company in Xiamen she was working within a familiar environment – she had spent her career with the company back home in Australia and understood the company's structure and processes. Her time in Xiamen involved familiar boundaries and Chinese employees of the company helped her with housing, shopping, visas and day-to-day necessities. After becoming redundant from the company during corporate cutbacks five years before the interview, she decided to stay on in Xiamen. At the time of the interview, however, she felt more socially isolated and had to learn to understand the city on her own. She explained:

> I felt really nervous because I was outside of the infrastructure of [the company]. They used to do everything for me. They registered me at

the local police station, you know, all those things in a foreign country were taken care of. So, slowly I started asking people, what do
I need to do to be here? Another [Western] friend who has been here
a long time, I mean, I was asking her daily questions. What do we do
now? It was hard. In fact, it was the first time I had to rely on others, other than myself...I had loads of questions. Who could I ask?
I could only talk to the other foreigners...The line between business and friendship is blurred here. Even for the foreign community.
One reason I try not to get too involved with the foreign community here is that that line can be terribly blurred and before you
know it can...you end up not talking to certain people or become
uncomfortable.

Marion's experience of being away from reliance on her employer
meant that despite having been in Xiamen for some time, she was
lacking the knowledge she needed to competently live and do business there. When she stepped out of this familiar corporate structure
she experienced the emotional structure of fear ('I felt really nervous
because I was outside of the infrastructure of the company'). To rectify
this vulnerability she felt as an individual in a different and 'illegible' environment, she needed to 'ask people, what do I need to do
to be here?' She had to seek knowledge and information from other
Westerners about how to 'cope with' her vulnerable position. She now
saw her relationships with other Westerners as dependent and necessary in order to successfully navigate the city ('For the first time I had
to rely on others, other than myself'). Outside of the familiar realm
of the corporation she worked for, she now had to rely on others
for knowledge about how to make sense of difference. At the same
time that these dependent relationships developed, Marion felt aware
that hierarchies of knowledge were being established and that she had
to be careful or wary of the unclear division between friendship and
business.

Marion was aware that interpersonal relationships held a different
dynamic than they did at home because of this dependency and knowledge hierarchy. She spoke about this notion of social interaction as
different to interaction at home, using a notion of risk to make the
distinction:

I made much more real friends here than I ever made in Australia.
Because in Australia it was *all* superficial. I stayed at home. I did my
vegetable patch. I went to work. I was in a stable world. It wasn't

volatile … I just did everything myself. And when I came here it was difficult because I had to talk with others and maybe I had to cooperate with others as well because you have to. It's ok to take but you have to give something first. That means, you put the effort in and you risk something, say a disagreement or a difference of opinion. You may have a fight about it. But then you have to say, ok, we're adults, we can get past it. There are some people who can't think this way … There are a number of foreigners who just use up your kindness. That's the way they do business. Using friendship. Using in the way that they are looking for the opportunities where they can benefit themselves, essentially. Especially those people who don't feel so sure of themselves in China and Xiamen and maybe they have no connection with anybody else. And so they see that as an opportunity. Here you are laying a lot more on the line [in a friendship]. Much more because people have to survive and if you are really having trouble, personally or business-wise, people get to know a lot about you and it really opens you up. It's different. You *need* people more and they need you more.

Marion was aware of the dependent nature of her relationships in Xiamen, and this reflexivity on her behalf led her to an awareness of emerging social rules about the giving and receiving of information. These social rules required a *co*-dependent relationship characterized by risk. Rather than the one-way exchange of information inherent in a dependent relationship, Marion became aware that within the community 'you had to give something first'. It was in relationship to the experience of vulnerability that this re-engagement with localized social structure took place. Marion observed how the perceived 'volatility' of the Xiamen environment led people to enter a relationship with other Westerners which involved both giving and taking of information, knowledge and support. Those who did not abide by these rules of reciprocity – those who Marion described as being 'unsure of themselves in China and Xiamen' – were considered not trustworthy because they were not willing to risk the giving of information as well as the accumulation of it.

The notion of 'risk' was central here to the link between the experience of vulnerability and the re-engagement with community and structure at the local level. The action of risking information and knowledge which would aid in processes of 'understanding' the local environment was to result in forms of both social connections (trust) and division (distrust). Marion recognized that these social conventions were necessary because the successful functioning of interpersonal relationships was a matter of 'survival' in this 'volatile' environment. Co-dependent relationships were characterized by this notion of risk. The social exchange of information was therefore calculated in terms of trust, status and division within the local community.

Such co-dependency was seen by many interviewees as different from friendships they held at home. Melissa described this heightened sense of dependency:

> There's a lot of networking that happens in China. The longer you are here as an expatriate, the more connections you make in the Chinese community as well as the foreign community. A lot of that networking is on both sides. Everybody is here for a different reason but sometimes those reasons tie you together in very unexpected ways. Business-wise, or just life-wise. So there is definitely a higher level of co-dependency as an expatriate – especially in as small a community as we have here in Xiamen. Shanghai, I think, would be much more... disconnected.

For Melissa, those who had been in China the longest had the most connections which she saw as holding value for others who might need them ('The longer you are here as an expatriate, the more connections you make'). The co-dependency she described was about the ability to 'get by' in business and in 'life' in an environment that was not as familiar as more cosmopolitan, global cities, such as Shanghai. This co-dependency was a means to palliate the experience of vulnerability. Without the common experiences of the emotional structures of anxiety, ecstasy and fear this co-dependent nature of relationships in Xiamen would not be as strong. Vulnerability, therefore, formed an important foundation upon which structured communities in Xiamen were established.

The process described here involved the development of social divisions connected to this local urban environment. It was through a process of understanding the unfamiliar and making the city useable that knowledge and skills acquired social currency. In this way, the rules of community re-engagement were continually reinforced and a hierarchy was constructed based on the value held in particular types of knowledge.

By developing the skills and knowledge to make Xiamen a site of familiarity, the Xiamener gained prestige and status in the community. The processes of gossip, rumour and secrets served to regulate behaviour and reinforce the emerging social conventions that governed the exchange of knowledge within dependent or co-dependent relationships.

The process of transformation described here relates to what Appadurai (1996: 182) terms the 'creation of context' or 'neighbourhood' from a meaningless experience of space. New arrivals in Xiamen, with little knowledge about how to deal with what was perceived to be a potentially threatening environment, experienced the city as *space* with no awareness of the deep and symbolic significance of places. They were unable to 'read' or make sense of the text of the city. In order to rectify the vulnerability this incurs, knowledge or ways of understanding must be developed. The previously illegible and rebellious space becomes a frame or a setting where human action can be initiated and conducted meaningfully. Xiamen became such a setting through the development of systems of trust and dependency. Appadurai (1996: 142) terms this the 'production of neighbourhood' in that space is transformed into a context or a set of contexts within which meaningful social action can be both generated and interpreted.

Rather than modern mobility leading to a 'general condition of creeping placelessness' (Relph in Cresswell 2004: 49), place is redefined by transient people, and as a result social structure and identity are also reconsidered and reconstructed in unfamiliar environments. This redefinition of self, place and community is made possible through the experience of vulnerability.

Community and consumption

As Xiameners developed ways to either understand difference or to familiarize it, they were also in a process of reconsidering their identity and how they were situated in relationship to Chinese culture, other Westerners in Xiamen and wider notions of home and the global. In other words, by negotiating concepts of difference and familiarity, Xiameners were reconsidering and reconstructing their own identities within broader structural and ideological boundaries. This claim is consistent with Malpas' (1999) link between the construction of subjectivity and the construction of place. He argues:

> Place is ... that within and with respect to which subjectivity is itself established – place is not founded on subjectivity, but is rather *that on which* subjectivity is founded. Thus, one does not first have a subject that apprehends certain features of the world in terms of the idea of

place, instead, the structure of subjectivity is given in and through the structure of place.

(Malpas 1999: 35)

In Xiamen, the re-establishment of subjectivity was concurrent with the processes of re-engagement with community. It was through reconsidering notions of familiarity and difference in the local environment that the conditions were set for this re-engagement.

However, concepts of familiarity and difference served to divide the community in terms of the degree to which the participants sought experiences or products which were deemed culturally familiar or different. The consumption of places and products which were understood as familiar or different was representative of the way a participant located themselves within the moral landscape. Likewise, this consumption indicated the emergence of further social divisions within the population, providing further evidence for the development of a new, yet nevertheless 'thickly' structured community.

A corridor of fairy-lights led the way towards The Mansion restaurant. It is rumoured that the colonial-era house used to be owned by an eccentric old French woman who kept company with a multitude of cats. The Mansion was bought by a foreign businessman some years ago and now stands as the city's most exclusive Western restaurant serving 'Contemporary Western Cuisine' and fine wines. The restaurant is somewhat hidden and, without knowledge of the city or a recommendation from others, it is almost impossible to find.

On the other side of town is the Tian Lai Bar. The dark and noisy room is full of young Chinese and a smattering of Westerners. Local beer is served with plates of cold green beans and salty fish. The young female bar staff speak little or no English yet keep the Western clientele smiling and communicate patiently with Chinese-language students. The live music can be hard to hear over the sound of a traditional dice game. The doors are open late and barbequed meat, cigarettes or fried rice can be ordered in from the surrounding small businesses.

The Mansion restaurant and the Tian Lai Bar are spatial representations of hierarchical divisions among the Western population based on perceptions of cultural difference and familiarity. The Mansion's Western clientele are business people – entrepreneurial traders, employees of large international firms and visiting business contacts. Tian Lai's Western clientele, on the other hand, are mostly English-language teachers and students. This division in the use of places in the city is reflected in the occupational stratification noted by Josie, a 27-year-old English teacher from Australia:

Tian Lai people don't want to be around The Mansion people. I mean, Tian Lai people will go on Thirsty Thursdays but the normal Mansion people will disappear then. It's probably about money why we go to Tian Lai then. The Mansion people think they're too good to go to Tian Lai. Unless they're drunk. The Mansion is like not being in China. The bar staff all speak English there and you can get mojitos and martinis if you want. You hardly ever see Chinese people there. At Tian Lai there are just as many, if not more Chinese there than Westerners. It's near the English schools so it's pretty handy for the teachers and students too. Teachers don't want to be at The Mansion. That's not what they want. They are going crazy, partying five nights a week. The Mansion is full of business people. We'd rather go somewhere where we can let our hair down. Teachers are having the same experiences as each other. You have the same bad-China-days but business people have different bad-China-days. They'd see our problems in China as being stupid…The Tian Lai crowd don't have that normal life.

For Josie, places in the city were used differently not only according to occupational class but also according to a common experience of the liminal period ('*We'd* rather go somewhere where *we* can let our hair down' and '*They* don't have that normal life') and common situatedness between the values of familiarity and difference ('The Mansion is not like being in China'). The emerging subgroups and their uses of places in the city were therefore linked to a common experience of vulnerability ('They have different bad-China-days'). The way the city was used by the different groups that emerged was indicative of divisions and solidarities made possible because of these vulnerable processes.

Dean (26, England) reiterated the division of subgroups in the city:

There are definitely different groups of foreigners here. You have the students, you have the teachers and you have the workers. There are definitely those groups. Not that they don't intermingle socially. They do. But they will go out together in those groups and stay in those groups. It's just like, we're here and we are doing the same thing.

Recent studies of Western migrants have highlighted a class system within contemporary expatriate communities (for example, Farrer 2010; Fechter and Walsh 2010). While Farrer (2010: 1223) claims this is most evident between highly paid foreign professionals and what he describes as 'often derided English teachers and corporate refugees', I suggest that in Xiamen such groups could be understood as more than occupational class divisions. Social bonds and divisions were based around differences in the degrees to which Westerners either sought cultural familiarity or cultural difference. Such divisions were maintained through the use of different sites (such as restaurants and bars) within the city itself, and the consumption of food and recreational space were markers of sub-groups within the community. Gail (59, US) explained these divisions by speaking about the consumption of food:

> Something that irritates me about expatriates is that they talk about, oh, I've got to go home and what will I fix for the children tonight – we have to have pizza or we have to have hamburgers – and I think, don't you ever go out for Chinese food? And they say, oh no, my children don't like it. I thought, if I am living in China and if I have children, they damned well better get used to Chinese food or learn to cook themselves. You're in China, for God's sake! ... I've met surprisingly many like that. They try to create the Western home. Everything is Western.

The relationship to China as *different* formed the basis of Gail's decision that she was not like certain other Westerners in the city who did not share her own relationship to cultural difference. The meaning that she attached to the consumption of familiar or different food represented her positioning of self within a wider moral landscape as a result of the processes of vulnerability. This mirrors Cronon's (1992: 32) assertion:

> When people exchange things in their immediate vicinity for things that can only be obtained elsewhere, they impose a new set of meanings on the local landscape and connect it to the wider world.

The 'new set of meanings' placed on food and its connection to the wider world reflected the moral landscape within which Gail operated. Gail's discussion about the consumption of food was in fact a discussion about her relationship with notions of 'home' and the 'West'. The use of concepts of 'Western' food and the creation of a 'Western' home meant that Gail had decided that what she is familiar with existed in opposition to what she experienced in the local environment in Xiamen. By consuming these familiar products, Gail considered that the social meaning of these things had changed in *this place*. The familiar had become de-contextualized and therefore, for Gail, devalued.

The division between people who sought different or familiar cultural experiences was further explained by Ben (63) from New Zealand:

> Some people are better at being international than others. There are two ways of looking at it. One is that people who consider themselves international can fit in anywhere and not be ethnocentric in how to deal with situations. Then there are other people who can survive on their own by protecting their personal space who also go anywhere and not be too adversely affected by it. There are these two different approaches. I am probably the isolationist one. But I wish I was the other. You create a bubble for yourself where you don't need the environment you are in. The alternative is someone who immerses themselves, cleaves and adapts to wherever they are. Some people probably couldn't do either. You have to learn to manage yourself.

Ben's example described the link between the experience of vulnerability and the resulting divisions which arise between Westerners as a result of 'learning ways to manage yourself'. He saw that divisions lie between those who could adapt to the different environment they were in and those who constructed 'a bubble of familiarity' so they 'don't need the environment they are in'. This concept of constructing a setting of 'Western-ness' in order to 'cope with' an unfamiliar cultural space was discussed by other participants such as Simon:

> Some people are very happy to live a very closeted life in China. Some people can live very happily, living outside the culture they are living in. Some people hide themselves away. They build a little wall around themselves and they have their own little part of England or their own little part of Australia or wherever they are from and they will feather their nest, feather their life with all the trappings of their home country. Once they leave the environment of that feathered nest, they feel either uncomfortable or frustrated. Some people will openly say they don't like it... I think some other Western people in China like to feel that they are involved in some weird fucked-up anthropological study that they've taken it upon themselves to do. And some of them are better at it than others. It's something that I wouldn't do actively because it's just not the kind of person I am.

By discussing the differences in the ways Westerners cope with difference and construct notions of familiarity, Simon was also discussing the formation of his own location within this environment. His own identity or subjectivity was being reconsidered, or reconstructed, at the same time that he was talking about the divisions in the Western community based on the use of place and vulnerability.

In Xiamen, certain products and places were recognized as Western and further had become symbolic of a relationship to local notions of place and to wider notions of globality. This symbolic relationship was the basis of a division within Xiamen between those who sought to discover what was familiar and attach to it, and those who sought to discover this notion of familiarity but yet wanted to distance themselves from it. This process of attachment or disconnection from notions of familiarity through consumption was the manifestation or performance of the process of the positioning of self within the moral landscape.

Relationships of division and connection were constructed through the negotiation of different understandings of place as a result of experiences of vulnerability. Gail, Ben and Simon's examples of divisions related to cultural familiarity and difference are representative of those who consider themselves to be in Xiamen independently of corporate or formal group structures. They each saw themselves as acting as an individual who was developing ways to 'cope with' an unfamiliar urban environment. They each considered themselves to belong to a group of Westerners who were also 'individuals' dealing with this process in a similar way.

These examples, therefore, provide exemplary cases of how the value of individualism is channelled through community and shared values. This suggests that postmodern claims that increasing global mobility results in a sense of heightened individualism and vulnerability need to be considered as part of wider contexts which continue to be framed within ongoing and dynamic structures and social divisions. An alternative, communal means for the construction of familiarity and difference was found in those who belonged to formal associations for Westerners.

Formal associations and groups

The International Christian Fellowship is held every Sunday morning in a hotel conference room. Passports are shown at the door and Chinese nationals are forbidden to take part. The room is full and a band begins to play contemporary English hymns and a projector screen displayed the lyrics for the 150 or so attendees. The service includes a sermon by an old-timer in Xiamen about how to not get angry and frustrated with those who upset you and ends with prayers in small groups. I link hands with the group of six people I have found myself sitting with, and participate in the activity as each member adds another item up for prayer.

The International Christian Fellowship was a formally organized and structured association. Regular activities included discussions about faith in China and the difficulties of living in Xiamen. For this group, dealing with vulnerability meant locating cultural difference within a familiar realm – that of Christian ideologies and beliefs. A note from my field diary describes the experience of attending the weekly Fellowship:

> I was surprised about the topics that people raised for prayer. One woman said 'I pray for people who don't know what love is. For all the orphaned babies who will never experience love'. The next said 'I pray for the Chinese government so that they will realize that a good society is a Christian society'. The prayers continued in this vein and at the end, the leader of the group invited people to come to the beach for English corner. He suggested that we talk to the Chinese children about Christianity and good values as a topic for their English lesson.
>
> (Field diary, 10 August 2005)

Attendees and members of the Fellowship were positioning themselves within the moral landscape with reference to organized Christianity. Familiar rites and rituals associated with their faith acted as temporal and ideological anchors around which the experience of vulnerability could be 'managed'. The experience of cultural illegibility was understood through the idea that the Chinese were somehow lacking the order and values of Western Christianity. The members of this group believed that if Christianity was embraced by the local Chinese population, then the city and its environment would seem less illegible to them. We have seen the way discourses of Western development and historical comparisons were a means to understand or legitimate perceived cultural and urban difference. For the Christian Fellowship, difference was explained through the absence of structured Christianity.

The Fellowship performed this 'conversation' about familiarity and difference together using common accepted language and regular activities such as meals, Bible classes and charity work with schools and hospitals. Their experience of Xiamen was within the familiar realm and structure of Christianity which, to them, was the key to positioning cultural difference within wider historical and global frameworks. Diane (33, US), a regular attendee at the Fellowship, explained:

> I go there because one thing when I'm travelling with my husband, we get placed in different countries, but when you can find a church you know it's going to be pretty much the same wherever you go.

The same beliefs, the same morals, sometimes even the same songs! It's also community. I make a lot of friends there. So no matter where we go, I first try to find the church. I can also talk to people there about recommendations for places to go. For example, we lived in Hong Kong before we moved here and I talked to the Pastor there about coming here and he gave me a contact name for this place. I know that when we move from here eventually, the people here will help me get in touch with people wherever we are going to so that really helps. The values here, you know, in Asia, can seem quite different so it's nice to touch base with that kind of familiarity. We can live anywhere. Everywhere is the same. As long as I have a church I feel like I can become a part of things and I feel less alone.

For Diane, the vulnerability she experienced in China was counteracted with the familiarity of the Fellowship. Her account of the 'values in Asia' seeming 'quite different' was juxtaposed with her feeling she could be mobile and maintain her value set provided she could connect with the structured familiarity of the group. This resonates with Williams' (1997) study of South Asian transnational religions in the United States which found that organized religious groups performed what was perceived as a protective function against what was most feared among the immigrant community – most notably a fear of the breakdown of values. The emotional structure of fear recounted in the previous chapter was challenged in this instance in a communal setting, using a familiarized institutional structure.

The International Christian Fellowship exemplified a structured group approach to vulnerability which reproduced social division with regard to the Chinese population and other Westerners who did not attach themselves to the group. Unlike Gail, Ben and Simon who renegotiated their identity in a more individual manner, the International Christian Fellowship members' experiences of belonging were based on a communal positioning within a moral landscape. This division between Westerners who perceive themselves as individualist and those who are a part of a group was explained by Ben:

There is a very strong Christian enclave of Westerners here. Very strong. I've not gotten into it but I hear about it. I'm sure they behave like normal Westerners. I'm not a group person. I don't get into groups. I flick in and out of them. I don't like being subjected to the decision making of a group...I go by myself and make decisions for me.

In this example, Ben was positioning himself within a moral landscape by considering himself in relation to those involved with the Christian Fellowship. Ben reaffirmed the value he places on individualism through positioning himself as not belonging to a group which he felt did not share this value. The presence of subgroups within the community was based around the reconsideration of the value oppositions which underpin globalism – individualism and the community, freedom and constraint, and familiarity and difference.

It was the experience of vulnerability which laid the foundations for the positioning of self within a moral landscape. Global mobility does not, therefore, result in the demise of place, structure and emotion. Rather, it is mobility itself and the resulting emotional structures of vulnerability that create the conditions which allow for the reconsideration and reconstruction of forms of identity and structure which remain bound by ideas of territoriality, community structure and belonging.

Conclusion

The vulnerable emotional structures (anxiety, ecstasy, fear) discussed in Part I facilitated attempts to understand what was perceived to be an illegible urban environment. This process was based around what Appiah (2006) termed 'conversations' between various value sets which underpin globalism – individualism/communalism, freedom/constraint and familiarity/difference. As the Westerners decided where they stood in relation to these conceptual poles, they were simultaneously positioning themselves within what has been termed here as a 'moral landscape'. In engaging with these conceptual conversations about such values, they were defining themselves and others *as* they were defining their relationship to their present locality, their homes and wider ideas of global values.

Authority was held by those who had the knowledge of place and who could influence others in their emerging understandings of the urban environment. Those who had been in Xiamen the longest and those with the necessary business and cultural knowledge were better placed to be in a position of authority as opposed to those who had recently arrived and were undergoing the liminal processes described. This hierarchy based on place and time knowledge was maintained and reinforced through the constant influx of new Westerners into the city.

The re-engagement with community and structure was regulated and maintained through gossip and rumour. Knowledge of the city and subsequent status hierarchies and divisions between subgroups meant that secrets also created a bond *and* a perceived risk for those immersed in a setting where business and friendship distinctions were not always clear. Local knowledge was a form of social currency governed by conventions and rules such as risk and trust. The emergence of a system of ranking, hierarchy, regulation, trust and social risk all indicated the presence of a localized community that was structured around renegotiated notions of cultural familiarity and difference.

Prominent community divisions at times resulted from 'value conversations' (Appiah 2006) between familiarity and difference. The consumption of symbolic familiarity or difference led to the creation of subgroups which identified themselves with shared notions of what it meant to be from the West. These divisions were further highlighted through the communal approaches to familiarity and difference in the example of the International Christian Fellowship.

The divisions formed in Xiamen were a result of differing reactions to the emotional structure of vulnerability. Such relationships between vulnerability and social structure demonstrate that the significance of the notions of postmodern rootlessness lies not as a final condition or consequence of increased global mobility. Rather, such experiences of rootlessness perform a valuable role in providing the necessary conditions for the recognition, reconsideration and reconstruction of place-bound forms of social structure.

Accordingly, this further reinforces the continued relevance of place and social structure for globally mobile people. Rather than global mobility resulting in ambivalent and free-floating cosmopolitans, a time of such vulnerability is necessary for the recreation and reconstruction of relatively 'thick' and 'hot' forms of community, solidarity and identity.

The formation of social structure and power is intimately linked with the construction of identity and belonging which stands between the micro-level of the local and the value systems which underpin globalism. Rather than global mobility resulting in what Turner (2000) claims to be 'thin' and 'cool' forms of identity and solidarity, global mobility provides the *conditions* for the reconsidering and reconstruction of changed yet still 'thick' and 'hot' forms of sociality.

6
Gender and Race

As these middling migrants engaged in the interpretation of place, they were concurrently repositioning themselves within a moral landscape and reconstructing the social norms and expectations that govern interaction. This process of re-attachment to social structure was only possible because of the experience of vulnerability which created the conditions for this to occur.

This chapter explores the construction and effects of power within this context. Gender and race are described here as linked social structures imbued with power dynamics which became visible through the processes of vulnerability. This visibility of structure led to the reconsideration and reconstruction of complex and sometimes conflicting local power relations. I follow Foucault's ([1976] 1988: 103) claim that 'sexuality is a dense transfer of power charged with instrumentality' and explore the links between such gendered power transfer and the social construction of racialized power.

Pierson (1998: 2) claims that 'the power relations of gender have intertwined with those of class, race and sexuality and that these technologies of power have been at the heart of the histories of imperialism, colonialism and nationalism shaping our modern world'. Contemporary constructions of these 'technologies of power' are located at the everyday, local level for those living global lives.

The term 'Western' is such a technology of power. The 'West' is, and remains, a racialized concept, often standing as a synonym for 'white' (Bonnett 2004). Postcolonial continuities within notions of the 'East' and the 'West' continue to function as bases for powerful forms of racial exclusion (Jackson 1998: 104). According to Fechter (2007) this is the case even – or especially – in settings where expatriates are ostensibly disinterested in a colonial past. This applies to Xiamen where Western transnational workers framed their presence in terms of contributing to the global future rather than expressing any form of continuity with a colonial past. Nevertheless, as Knowles (2005: 107) argues, 'empire survives as a feeling of choice and opportunity, (divergent forms of entitlement, facilitated by a (racialized) geography of routes already carved out by others'. It is in exploring the experience of 'feeling' – here conceptualized in terms of emotional structures – associated with ideas of choice that both the ruptures and the continuities between postcoloniality and globality become apparent. Rather than globalization resulting in a distinct new era of social relations, global mobility creates the conditions for both the reaffirmation of historically constructed power dynamics and the possibility for challenging these very same discourses.

Since the 1990s there has been an increased interest in gender relations within studies of skilled migration. This is a result of a recognition within academia that until recently ethnographic studies of mobile people which have approached gender as a variable have tended to focus primarily on the feminization of unskilled migration (Kofman 2000; Willis and Yeoh 2002). While unskilled and dependent migration had been 'feminized', skilled and individual migration was masculinized within migration research. The international skilled migrant was perceived to be the single person, usually assumed to be male, disembodied and disembedded from contexts such as familial or household relationships or the wider society in which he lives (Findlay et al. 1996; Hardill 1998). This bias has begun to be rectified in a recent academic push towards conceptualizing privileged migrant women as occupying diverse roles within global contexts and viewing the migrant as embedded within local contexts (see, for example, Brooks and Wee 2008; Fechter 2007, 2010; Fechter and Hindman 2011; Leonard 2010a and 2010b; Yeoh and Willis 2005; Walsh 2006, 2012).

Likewise, studies of notions of race as associated with 'whiteness' and 'Western-ness' have been historically underrepresented in skilled migration research (Fechter and Walsh 2010). As Bonnett (1997: 1993) argues, 'whiteness'

> remains a relatively under-discovered and under-researched 'racial' identity ... While the history and categorization of non-whiteness has been frequently subject to debate, it is only in the past few years that a comparable discussion has begun on the subject of whiteness. One of the most important consequences of this relative invisibility has been the naturalization of whiteness for white people.

While these conceptual invisibilities remain at a disciplinary level (Fechter and Walsh 2010: 1198), there does exist a growing interest in the area from what has been termed the 'Third Wave' of whiteness scholarship (Bonnett 2008; Twine and Gallagher 2008). Third-wave whiteness 'acknowledges the relational, contextual and situational ways in which white privilege can be at the same time a taken-for-granted entitlement, a desired social status, a perceived source of victimization and a tenuous situational identity' (Twine and Gallagher 2008: 7).

It has been the influence of feminist deconstructionist work which has led to this emphasis on the personal and the political and the articulation of power and oppression (Hunter, Swan and Grimes 2010: 411). As studies of gender and privileged migration increase in number, so too do studies that take into account whiteness as an imagined geography of power (see, for example, Armbruster 2010; Fechter 2005, 2010; Fechter and Hindman 2011; Knowles 2005; Korpela 2010; Leggett 2005, 2010; Leonard 2008, 2010a). Nevertheless, this field remains in its infancy and important questions about the relationships between social structure and contemporary meanings behind the idea of the 'West' are still to be answered.

This chapter focuses on the context of Xiamen, and how interpretation of a perceived 'illegible' urban space is done together with the construction of geographies of gendered and racialized power. Mahler and Pessar (2006: 42) ask:

When the geographical spaces we study extend across international borders, does this multiplication and dispersal produce even greater opportunities for the reinforcement of prevailing gender ideologies and norms, or, conversely, do transnational spaces provide openings for men and women, girls and boys, to question hegemonic notions of gender [and] to entertain competing understandings of gendered lives?

Gendered and racialized discourses were sought within the interview narratives which either reinforce the norms of 'home' or question these same norms. Notions of 'Western-ness' and masculinity and 'Western-ness' and femininity were constructed concurrently. Rather than globalization resulting in what Beck and Bauman describe as condition of 'rootless' cosmopolitanism, such 'rootlessness' functions to allow gendered and racialized structures to continue to be created and contested within contextualized boundaries.

It should be noted here that, in addressing the intersection between gender and race in Xiamen, these categories of meaning are far from universal. Invoking gender and race as significant structural considerations by no means pre-supposes that the experiences of transnationality are common to *all* men or *all* women. Nor does it presuppose that the experiences of 'Chinese-ness' and 'Western-ness' are homogenous. Instead, what these analytical tools signify is the multiple and contradictory meanings attached to sexual and racial difference, and how these multiplicities continue to 'shape and influence the way people live their daily lives and how they think about the world around them' (Levine 2004: 2; see also Leonard 2010; Scott 1999: 25). First, I explore the construction of notions of Western masculinities.

Considering Western masculinities

The interview with Greg had been going well. We'd been chatting for over an hour and it seemed he was enjoying the chance to explain his life and his experiences. Now, however, I was asking him about differences between the way Western women and Western men experience Xiamen. He shifted in his seat and paused, awkwardly. 'Do I have to answer that?' he pleaded. 'You know what I mean?' He laughed and suggested instead that we discuss the weather in Toronto.

After some thought, Greg eventually explains what he meant. 'Well, ok, yes. I do think there is a difference between the ways Western men and women experience Xiamen in a way. You see here quite often 70-year-old Western men with 20-year-old girlfriends which would never happen at home'. He leans forward, as if he is telling me something in confidence. 'I mean, it happens to superstars. Maybe Clint Eastwood could do it. But for the ordinary Joes like me and those guys, that would never happen in our culture'.

The hesitancy of Greg and many other Western men who were interviewed for this research to respond to questions about gender differences was strongly in contrast with Western women, who spoke often at length about gender issues. It became clear that it was my own position as a Western female that was prompting both the hesitation of Western men to speak about gender with me and the openness of Western women to do the same. My belonging to a gendered and racialized group clearly influenced the way in which people interacted with me.

In these situations it was apparent that such conversations were not only about my gender but also about my being 'Western'. Stephen (29) from the United States, for example, answered my question about different gendered experiences for Westerners in Xiamen by speaking from the perspective of his friend:

> An American girl I know, she said, you men are great in Chinese girl's eyes. It's easy. You love it because of all the girls here. I didn't realize that before and so I said, have you never fancied a Chinese guy? And she said never, it never happens. I said really? I don't know, I don't watch men so I don't really know about that.

As a male, Stephen felt he wasn't in a position to speak about gendered differences. Like Greg, there was hesitancy in his response. Nevertheless, Stephen clearly separated four groups of people within this short quote – the 'American girl', 'Chinese girls', 'Chinese guys' and himself – distinct from other categories as both a male and Western. During such interviews with Western men, I often felt I was asking inappropriate questions about the inside dealings of a group of which I wasn't a member.

Despite the hesitancy of some Western men to speak openly gender differences, their responses suggested that it was in response to the vulnerability that notions of gender and race were reconsidered. It was in the process of interpreting difference that gender became 'racialized' and race became 'genderized'. For example, when asked about the differences between the experiences of Western men and women, Bill from New Zealand reverted to comparing what he perceived as different notions of gender for Chinese women:

> Oriental women have a different sense of personal space than Western women. They are more likely to put up with the situation as their loss. But what Western women do is they simply change the situation. Western women are more in your face. The Chinese woman is likely to be more passive.

In recounting his perceptions of women in Xiamen, gender became a racial category that was linked to perceived values. For Bill, gender was different for the Chinese women because they placed a different value on 'personal space' and on promoting change. Chinese or 'Oriental' femininity was constructed within Bill's quote as passive and submissive. Constructions of this ideal of Chinese femininity as different from Western femininity served to support or reinforce historically constructed ideas of 'legitimate' gender roles and relationships where Western men were dominant and authoritative.

Such gendered and racialized geographies echo accounts from postcolonial studies and colonial histories which recount the masculine processes of conquering and 'civilizing' a feminine East (Levine 2004; Said 1978). Said (1978) concluded that Western writings about the 'Orient' depicted it as an irrational, weak, feminized 'Other', contrasted with the rational, strong, masculine West, a contrast he suggested derives from the need to create value-laden 'difference' between West and East. Clancy-Smith and Gouda's (1998) study of French and Dutch imperial language showed that colonial language depicted the colonies as feminine, virgin land awaiting virile young European men. This gendered vocabulary 'infused political rhetoric in Europe and in Europe's colonies, and it transplanted culturally specific understandings of gender into new environments' (Clancy-Smith and Gouda 1998: 17). The 'Orient' became represented in feminine metaphors equated with sexual desire, nature, the body and the uncivilized (Said 1978). This 'Othering' of the Orient served to legitimate the white man's perceived superiority over both the non-white and the non-male world.

Contemporary feminist writings on women in Asia argue that these imperial stereotypes continue to be constructed today. Prasso (2005: 1) writes of Western men in Asia that 'their very literal passion attributes to identifying Asian with "the feminine", and assigning the region and its people attributes that are typically associated with femininity in the West'. She argues that casting Asia as sexual and dangerous is what has drawn the eyes of the West to the East for centuries, and this continues to be the case. Asian women, she says, are today perceived in the West as servile, passive and mystical (Prasso 2005; also see Manderson and Jolly 1997).

The historical construction of 'Oriental' femininity as hyper-feminine was present within many interview narratives. Western femininity, on the other hand, was constructed as the alternative – dominant, empowered and threatening. For example, in Bill's quote above, he described Western women as able to 'simply change the situation' and describe them as 'more in your face'. This notion of an active Western femininity in contrast to a passive Chinese femininity was in some cases reaffirmed by Western women. For example, Sarah explained what she considered Western men to value in Chinese women:

> So, I think the [Western] men, maybe they can have a beautiful girl, a beautiful Chinese girl, very feminine – they're so feminine here. The Western men love the fact that they dress so feminine – they take care of their hair, their nails and it goes on.

Chinese women were constructed by both Western men and Western women within such discourse as symbolizing and embodying difference. This difference was embodied in the re-evaluation of the white female body 'vis-à-vis an idealised Asian female body' (Fechter 2007: 73). The Chinese woman was seen as representative of a version of an Other femininity which, in this case, was constructed as passive, subservient and exotic as opposed to a masculinized Western femininity.

A moral repositioning was often constructed around a notion of an 'immoral' Chinese masculine 'Other'. Chinese women were often spoken about by Western men as being 'saved' from immoral and harsh gender relationships in the Chinese ('Other') culture. For example, Craig explained:

> It seems to be that Chinese females are more open to trying to find someone that's *laowai* [Western] than they are trying to find someone that's Chinese. I've watched, you know, and I can see that Chinese men are pretty mean to Chinese women. They treat them like they are supposed to be a king and they're supposed to wait on them hand and foot and I think there is a lot of adultery that goes on with a Chinese man. You see that a lot. I know factory owners that are married and they have two or three other girlfriends, you know. That's something I never did think much of.

Craig was here in a process of repositioning himself within a moral landscape that was at once gendered and racialized. He described Chinese men as 'pretty mean' to Chinese women and referred to the perceived immoral behaviour of these 'Other' men (as adulterous and exploitative). In doing so, Craig was separating himself from the Chinese male 'Other' at a moral level ('That's something I never did think much of'). This emotional structure of fear became the basis for a gendered and racialized reconsideration of the moral landscape.

The perception of cultural difference within gender relations led to the construction of Chinese masculinity as immoral or dangerous and in such cases served to revalidate what were seen as 'Western' values. In trying to make sense of difference, these Western men were rectifying the emotional structure of fear using familiar moral terms. This finding resonates with Levine's (2004) argument that colonizers gauged how 'civilised' they considered a society to be through making a judgement about that society's treatment of women. Levine (2004: 6) argued that

such representations were themselves what we would call masculin-
ist, for they assumed that a critical function of society was to care
for and protect women, an idea which logically secured that women
would be defined by men and compared against male behaviours.

In the case of Xiamen, discourse about 'saving' Chinese women from
the 'immoral' Chinese man was a continuance of such discursive power
relations which served to reposition Western men as dominant.

Kim's (2006: 520) study of white men in Korea asserted that 'the
dominance of white masculinity depends on a subordinate non-white
masculinity'. The subordination of the non-white male was produced
through the negotiation of what has been termed in this book 'structures of vulnerability'. In order to create legibility in the environment,
the racialized and gendered 'Others', in particular Chinese men, were
positioned as subordinate or morally inferior – a claim which was
demonstrated through their perceived treatment of Chinese women.

This interpretation of difference involved the reconstruction of technologies of power. Gender and race became structures which were linked
to values associated with 'The West' (such as individualism, equality and
freedom) (see Hunter, Swan and Grimes 2010: 408). These two structures
therefore became a discursive location for the reaffirmation of these
perceived values. Roger from Canada referred to such conceptual links
between values, gender and race:

> We treat them [Chinese women] better than Chinese men do. They
> [Chinese women] like us because we treat them as equals.

Chinese men were 'Othered' with regard to both their gender and their
race in the positioning of the Western male self within the moral landscape. For Roger, the Western man valued universal equality, as opposed
to a non-Western, 'less moral' masculinity. A notion of an ideal moral
order of 'The West' was invoked to understand or make 'legible' what
was perceived as a moral difference.

The linking of concepts of masculinity and Western-ness is an effect of
a relationship of power resulting from a system of moral differentiation.
By making moral distinctions between Chinese femininity and Western
femininity and between Chinese masculinity and Western masculinity,
the Western man was reasserting his perceived position at the apex of
both a gendered and racial hierarchy. The production of such discourse
helped to maintain values associated with 'home'.

There was also a sense that this version of patriarchal values were
out-dated at home and that some Western men were, through their

discourse of gendered moral differentiation, recreating a version of masculinity that existed in a previous era in the West. John from the United States explained this perspective:

> I think Western men feel very comfortable here. It's very pleasing for them, I guess. I can only speculate though. And it's not all men. It's like they are trying to be the 1950s man-of-the-house thing. Like they are trying to step back in time to when men were men. It's like a boy's club here sometimes.

We have seen how narratives of linear development were often employed by Westerners in Xiamen to interpret difference. Here, John was making sense of the illegible by relating what he perceived as gender differences to historical time frames of the West. It was the experiences of vulnerability that facilitated this reconsideration of gendered and racialized discourse.

Others perceived the construction of Western patriarchy in Xiamen as being an exaggerated version of continuing gender relationships at home. For some Western women, the processes of vulnerability allowed for the gendered power at home to become more visible. Bethany from the United States reflected on this:

> It's the man/woman thing but then you bring it here to China and you exaggerate it. It's more exaggerated. It's the same as back home but you don't notice it because you have to live by society's rules. But here, it seems, it's all open.

The processes of vulnerability allowed Bethany to become aware of power relationships at home. In a different and distanced urban environment, she was able to reconsider the gender 'rules' which constituted her social life at home. Vulnerability allowed both Western men and women to reconsider gender roles and values of 'home'. The effect was a renegotiation of Western gendered relationships whereby Western men were in some cases able to reaffirm or legitimate Western patriarchal power relationships through their construction of notions of passive Asian femininities and immoral Asian masculinities.

Considering Western femininities

Josie arrives in Xiamen for the first time at 10.30 pm on a Monday night. Her friend from home picks her up from the airport and they go straight to a bar and sit down for a chat. Before long, other Westerners introduce themselves and the night continues into a warm summer haze. Miranda, an old-timer and hence at the top of the emerging hierarchy discussed in the previous chapter, sits next to her and toasts the new arrival. 'There is one important thing you need to know, though' she says. 'Don't expect to get any attention from men over here. Ever. Western men don't flirt with Western women. They all have the fever. You'll either get used to it or you'll leave'. Other women in the group nod in agreement while Josie, fresh off the plane from Sydney, laughs nervously.

Eighteen months later, I met Josie again. She was still in Xiamen and the knowledge of place she has accumulated through her time in Xiamen has led to her re-engaging with a system of status and hierarchy in the community. For example, at this point she was a member of a subgroup of friends that frequented regular places in town; she was aware of the hierarchies and gossip networks within the Western community and was adept and navigating the urban environment. I asked her about the differences between gendered experiences in the city. She explained:

> We're like a third gender over here. Western women, I mean. There are the men, there are the Chinese women who they see as being really feminine and soft and then there is us. We're not like women here. It's like the men think we are one of them and they expect us to keep up with their drinking, be one of the boys, listen to their worries about their Chinese girlfriends. But then, we're not really allowed to join them as well. It takes a lot of getting used to, the way they are.

Josie's account of her changed perceptions of gender during her time in Xiamen reflects the hyper-feminization of the Chinese women discussed in the previous section and suggests that one consequence is a 'masculinization' of Western women.

This changed perception of what it meant to be female was recounted by many Western women in Xiamen. While most Western men were perceived to be only interested sexually in Chinese women, Western women perceived that they were remote from the sexual gaze of both Western and Chinese men. Farrer's (2011) study of global nightscapes in Shanghai also found that Western women complained that they were ignored by foreign men and Chinese men and as a result felt 'desexualized' while in China.

In Xiamen, the de-sexualization of Western women often led to a reconsideration of gendered roles and expectations at home and sometimes a sense of liberation from what were seen as dependent gender relationships at 'home'. This perceived freedom from sexual structures contributed to the experience of ecstatic liminality after arriving in Xiamen. Gail, from New York, for example, reflected that:

> The life of a Western woman is most definitely different from a Western man. You make your own life. This is one place you don't depend on a man for anything. There aren't any!

This quote demonstrates that the experience of liminality was a gendered experience. Gail felt a sense of liberation from gendered norms and expectations and she implied that Western men underwent a different experience of vulnerability than Western women.

Marion also felt that a heightened sense of freedom was also a gendered experience:

> I know that women have their freedoms at home now and so on...but you know, if you're here you can just go around and you can just be yourself.

The perceived lack of sexual attention from both Western men and Chinese men and the concurrent construction of a Chinese hyper-femininity contributed to some Western women recounting a sense of independence, awareness and resistance against gender-based power relationships and identities at 'home'. This effect of changed discourses on gender and a shifting sexual gaze was seen by some Western women to be difficult, but nevertheless vital for 'survival' in Xiamen. Sarah described the emotional skills that were needed to negotiate this shift in gender relationships:

> As a woman, you have to have better self-confidence. You have to have more self-confidence as a woman to live here long term. A lot of women come here and last three months or six months because they just can't handle. It's too strange. It's not the society or the social life they're used to. They're unhappy and they just go home. You don't get the day-to-day attention...the flirtation...its amazing how much we complain about flirtation but how much that actually serves our ego on a day-to-day basis...You have to have a lot more self-confidence to live here in the long term. Men, whether they are fat, ugly, thin, whatever – are still given that attention. That confir- mation. That image confirmation on an everyday basis. No matter what they look like. But women get that much less – from Western men, hardly ever, and never from Chinese men.

In this quote, Sarah was describing the processes of vulnerability in terms of the emotional structure of fear ('It's just too strange. It's not the society they're used to'), the result of which was a necessary reconsideration of gendered expectations and norms. In order to 'cope' in the 'illegible' environment, women needed to change the way they considered themselves as gendered ('You have to have more self-confidence as a woman').

The perceived lack of a sexual gaze led women to feel that in order to negotiate the illegible landscape they needed to reconstruct their gendered identity. Sally, from Australia, described this reconstruction of gendered power relationships for both Western men and women:

> The men are building their confidence and the women are losing it. It makes you focus more on your personality and your skills and your abilities and much less on the clothes that you are wearing and how you look...Men tend to get arrogant and women tend to get...you don't see women getting arrogant in a sexual way in China, but you do see men getting arrogant in a sexual way. You do see women getting much more forceful, aggressive though. Because you have to.

Sally was reconsidering what it meant to be Western and female. This process was intimately an emotional experience. For Sally, women and men were shifting their emotional responses to gender difference ('Men tend to get arrogant...Women get much more forceful and aggressive'). These perceived changes to gendered emotional behaviour were seen as necessary for the successful negotiation of the 'illegible' environment ('Because you have to'). This gendered experience of emotional action supports Svasek and Skrbis' (2007: 374) suggestion that 'both male and female migrants are prone to experience a sense of emotional destabilization as their emotional dispositions, learned "back home", may not be acceptable in their new locations'. As the meanings of both gender and race were perceived differently in Xiamen than they were at home, so too were definitions of appropriate gendered emotional dispositions shifting in this new environment.

Femininity was considered by many Western women as a set of expectations and values that were different for Chinese women and for Western women. In this way, Western women were also intimately involved in the construction of gendered and racialized difference. Being a woman that was 'Western' meant developing the ability to deal with de-sexualization. While Farrer's (2011) study of Westerners in Shanghai claimed that Western women avoided the bar scene in order to 'avoid the sight of Western men hunting or being hunted by Chinese women' (p. 760), I did not find this to be the case in Xiamen.

Instead, Western women were involved in developing such skills that were spoken about as self-confidence, forcefulness and 'being one of the boys' (26, Australia). These traits were similar to those spoken about by Western men as being opposed to notions of the ideal passive femininity constructed in the notion of the Chinese woman. Femininity was hence being reconsidered around new discursive boundaries of 'Western-ness' and 'non-Western-ness'. Power relationships between Western men and Western women were also renegotiated as a result of shifting meanings of gender roles and identities.

This perceived de-sexualization of Western women contributed to the differentiation of Chinese women as passive and sexual and the Western woman as aggressive and asexual. Western men and Western women in Xiamen were actively involved in defining these differences in terms of gendered and racialized meanings. This finding supports Yoshihara's (2003) argument that 'white women played pivotal roles in inscribing gendered meanings to Asia, both complicating and replicating the dominant Orientalist discourse founded upon the notion of "West = Male vs. East = Female" '. While the construction of this passive (Asian) femininity and the immoral (Asian) masculinity reinforced the white male position of gendered and racial power, white women held a key role in this reconstruction and served to both legitimate and resist historical constructions of gendered and racialized power dichotomies.

While the perceived de-sexualization of Western women was spoken about mainly by single and unmarried women, a shift in gendered identities was also relevant for those who were in couples or who were married upon arrival in Xiamen.

Trailing spouses and married life

Janet, Kathy and Barbara came rushing through the door of the air-conditioned coffee shop, half an hour later than the time we'd agreed on, but full of apologies and explanations. 'We just had to see the new pearl shop on Zhong Shan Street', they explained, smiling and excited. 'You'd never believe the prices – it's incredible!' The three women unloaded their treasure on the table and we admired and compared colours and sizes until their coffees arrived. They'd each agreed to speak to me at the Association for Xiamen Expatriates luncheon I had attended but refused to consider being interviewed separately. 'We always do things together during the day', Janet said. 'Its easier like this sometimes and we have a lot of fun'. It seemed my group interview was a social activity for the three Australian wives of employees of a major multinational company.

As we chatted about where to buy the best fabric, get clothes tailored, buy fresh vegetables and get the best domestic help, it became clear that these women were a source of valuable information about the city. This knowledge about the city was shown in the previous chapter to hold social currency and to be the basis for connection and division in the local Western community. They were skilled at negotiating urban landscapes with little or no knowledge of Chinese language and were adept at creating a 'Western home' – a zone of meaningful cultural familiarity – in what was seen as a different urban environment. Janet explained:

> We are the ones who have to deal with the culture and have to get around the place. We come in contact with China a lot more than our husbands do. They go to work every day and it's similar to what it is at home. They speak English all day; work with their company just as they would at home. Then they come home and it's almost like they're not in China at all sometimes! But we have our days to fill. We have to get around, go shopping and things. Sometimes it's like we are living in China and they aren't.

For these women, their role in Xiamen extended to negotiating the urban landscape in order to produce familiarity for their husbands and children. The wife/mother role now extended to being in the 'front line' of interpreting the city and its places. This was seen as radically different from the experience of their husbands who worked within familiar Western corporate structures ('Sometimes it's like we are living in China and they aren't').

The interpretation of the 'illegible' urban environment was seen to be gendered work for these women. The domestic role of the wife and mother extended to include interpretation and negotiation of the city and the creation of cultural familiarity. Leonard (2008) also found that for British women in Hong Kong, gender differences were very apparent in discourses of maintaining links with the old 'home' and reproducing those links in the new context, are 'mainly feminine responsibilities and a key part of many feminine identities' (p. 50). For the women in Xiamen, this gendered responsibility involved the creation of zones of familiarity within the domestic sphere. For these women, it is the husband's paid work that brings the family into a situation of difference and it is the woman's work to erase the move (Hindman 2008).

At home, in Australia, these women considered the care of the home and food preparation as a part of their gender-based responsibilities. In Xiamen, however, all corporate expatriate wives (and many singles)

I interviewed employed domestic help. The employment of an *ai yi* (literally translated as 'auntie') was not only expected of most expatriate homes but was the basis of many conversations and gossip within the 'trailing-spouse' community. The *ai yi* would clean the house, often shop for groceries and household goods and in many cases would prepare meals for the family. The Western housewife, then, did not need to perform her daily domestic tasks as she would at home.

This 'version' of the expatriate woman resonates with images of the colonial wife who came in little contact with the local population and whose role it was to assuage the 'fear and anxiety' (Hindman 2008; Yeoh and Willis 2005) associated with living in a different environment. Fechter (2010) suggests little has changed in the expatriate context from that of their colonial predecessors as expatriate wives 'find themselves in a similar position to colonial women insofar as their support work is necessary and expected of them' (p. 43).

At first I had hypothesized that these Western corporate wives also fit the colonial stereotypes of the white woman. This was partly the result of what Knapman (1986) describes as two predominant stereotypes of the Western woman in the colonies. First, the morally upright, good-living and self-sacrificing pioneer and, second, the lazy, bored, spirit-drinker who was unable to cope with 'tropical weather and the conditions of life, and was in constant battle with irresponsible servants' (Knapman 1986: 14). These two stereotypes of white women as either idle or moralistic were brought together in colonial accounts of snobbery, self-indulgence, frivolity and indolence (Knapman 1986). My initial observations connected with a sense of boredom and idleness that perhaps echoed these colonial stereotypes. An entry from my field diary explains:

> After talking to the women at the Expatriate Women's club it became really clear to me that these women were bored. Many of them have had to give up their jobs at home – apparently a lot of TNCs insist on the spouse agreeing not to work in China as a stipulation of their contract. I guess that's why they all comfortably refer to themselves as 'trailing spouses'. They get an allowance from the company to support them according to the career they've given up at home. But they also don't need to do anything around the house – the *ai yi* does it all. All the cooking, cleaning, clothes washing. So for many of these women, the two fundamental aspects of their role, their identity – working woman and house-wife – have become redundant. I guess that's why they get out to these lunches and things together. To have

other people to talk to and to get help with dealing with all those changes.

(Field diary, 4 June 2005)

On further reflection, rather than frivolous or bored, I came to understand that the colonial-era resonation told only part of the story. Indeed, these women were undergoing profound changes with regard to their gendered identities and were engaging in new gendered work – most notably, the navigation and creation of a legible city landscape. Far from indolent or timid, these women were at the forefront of deciphering the urban and negotiating perceptions of difference and familiarity.

These women were finding their gendered identity changing in Xiamen with regard to their roles and expectations. Instead of working either in paid employment or within the domestic sphere, they were learning to understand the local landscape. Interpreting the city, rather than tending to the home, for these women was a part of their gendered and racialized expectations and experiences. They often performed these tasks together with other women in similar circumstances. In this way, the interpretation of the unfamiliar and different urban environment was conducted within boundaries of familiarity. Such interpretation and negotiation of vulnerability became, to a large extent, gendered work. Social bonds were produced with other women based on this process of reconsidering gender identity and the negotiation of vulnerability.

For both single women and married corporate wives, gender was renegotiated in tandem with the deciphering of what was perceived to be an illegible city. Single women, however, often regarded the 'trailing spouse' group as representative of gendered identities and relationships at 'home'. Single women, undergoing processes of perceived de-sexualization discussed earlier in this section, considered themselves dealing with different issues than those in marriages. Sally explained the different experiences for single women and those in a marriage:

> Those women who don't marry, they can find a satisfactory life . . . but some just leave Xiamen because they can't deal with it. But it's just part of single life here. It just seems that – I'm not trying to generalize – but single women who stay on here are of a particular character. You have to be to survive this place. You just have to accept that and say, I accept that . . . For some of the women here it becomes really isolated. I think some of them have to question their own values because they might have to compromise themselves. And then they might do things they might not do at home. There is such

a variety of people you can choose from at home – you can be a lot more picky – you don't have to see that side of life if you don't want to. But here there are just a few groups of people – the corporate couples and families and then there's the renegades.

Sally used the term 'renegades' throughout her interview to describe single people who were in Xiamen usually to start their own business or who work for a small company. This group of 'individuals' were considered by Sally as different from corporate couples and families who were considered to be negotiating vulnerability as part of a familiarly structured group. Being a single woman, for Sally, meant being 'isolated' and 'questioning her own values'. This heightened sense of individualism was linked with an awareness of gendered power relations. For such individuals it was then necessary to reconsider and 'question' the values associated with gendered social structure. Sally spoke here about not only this 'questioning' of values but also 'compromising' with regard to gendered action and expectations (such as greater participation than at home in excessive drinking, watching and participating in sport and forming relationships with men that they possibly wouldn't at home).

Further, this gendered reflexivity was a part of an experience of liminality. Sally conjectured that being outside of gendered social structure might lead people to 'do things they might not do at home'. She considered this gendered experience of vulnerability as part of her 'individualized' experience of difference and separated it from those who had arrived as a member of a 'couple'. Couples and families functioned for Sally as a cultural 'reminder' or a form of moral 'grounding' that she felt she sometimes needed:

> Sometimes, what I like to do is I like to keep friends with people in corporate families. It's stabilizing. It grounds you. It just sort of brings you back without being completely sucked into this, kind of, other world. You have to step out of it. And the only way to step out of it is to have a variety of friends – those with families and some singles that have a life like they would at home.

By being in an environment where gender roles and identities were familiar, Sally felt the experience of vulnerability was 'reigned in' or 'stabilized' within the perceived moral order of home. Away from such familiarity, she felt she was within a precarious environment where a 'particular character' was needed for a woman to 'survive'. This 'moral order' of home was both gendered and racialized and consisted of a continuation of historical discourses of marriage and monogamy as 'indicators of modernity' (Clancy-Smith and Gouda 1998).

Through gendered experiences of vulnerability, women and men were undergoing complex and sometimes contradictory renegotiations of gendered roles and expectations. Vulnerability led to an awareness of gendered social structures and meant that the power relationships between men and women in Xiamen were also being renegotiated. Some Western men were found to reaffirm a position at the apex of both a perceived gendered and racialized hierarchy while some Western women were found to be undergoing a process of both constructing and resisting these same value hierarchies.

While Western women were undergoing a process of reconsidering their gendered moral landscape, they nevertheless came to represent the disciplinary moral 'gaze' of home. These conflicting experiences demonstrated the ongoing relevance of place, structure and emotion for global lives and the potential for mobilities to create spaces for both contestation and creation of historicized power relations. While certain aspects of gender relations were destabilized, other aspects were further entrenched (Brooks and Wee 2008; McNay 1999: 103).

Gender relations

Every Sunday in Xiamen, a group of Western men meet at a golf club about an hour's drive from the city. After 18-holes they head back to the pub for a beer and recount the day's form and plan the next event.

The Xiamen Golf Society established itself as a formal association during my fieldwork and printed membership rules, regulations and merchandize. At the inaugural Annual General Meeting, however, the first crisis arose. Simon explained:

> There were two issues we were asked to vote on that people had been talking about. The inclusion of Chinese men into the society and the inclusion of Western women. It caused huge problems at the AGM. Everyone was divided and upset. In the end it was decided that Chinese men could be allowed in if they spoke sufficient English and maybe had an overseas education – they had to be acceptable to the members. But on the women thing . . . the guys just said no. There was only one man who wanted it and it was probably so his girlfriend could play but everyone else said no. The Western woman thing was a much bigger controversy in the meeting than I ever would have

thought it would be. They suggested that if women want to play they can come for special social events or start their own club.[1]

The Chinese men and the Western women were categorized in this example as the 'Other' who threatened the existing moral order of this white male group. Chinese women were absent altogether from the discussion. The formation of exclusive white male domains such as the Golf Society was a reaction to both the structures of vulnerability and was a means of creating boundaries to reinforce and maintain the white, male position at the perceived top of both gendered and racialized hierarchies.

Western women, likewise, found means to assert power in relationship to those they saw as threatening to the perceived values of 'home'. Language was used between Western women to refer to Western men who were seen to be breaking the moral codes of home in their relationships with the Other feminine. The term *xiao jie* was used to refer to waitresses and also to prostitutes in the Xiamen region. Some Western women in Xiamen occasionally referred to a Western man's Chinese girlfriend, or any young Chinese woman who appeared interested in Western men, as a *xiao jie*. This derogatory use of language was a means of resistance to both the perceived immoral behaviour of Western men and the 'Other' hyper-femininity embodied by Chinese women. Invitations to events organized by Western women (such as parties, boat excursions or outings) were sometimes attached to a caveat that *xiao jie's* were not welcome. Western women were attempting to create racialized and gendered boundaries in order to create a position of power over the 'Other' femininity.

These examples uncover an essential contradiction between competing notions of the moral structure of the West. Kim's (2006: 520) research described Korean women as viewing hegemonic white masculinity as heroic, gender egalitarian and gender progressive. This perception of white men as gender progressive was used in contrasting ways by both Western women and Western men in Xiamen. While Western men sometimes perceived themselves as demonstrating progressive ideals in their relationships with Chinese women (that is, in 'saving' them from supposed oppressive Chinese gender relations), Western women perceived white male relationships with Chinese women to be the opposite: gender oppressive, repressive and exploitative.

These competing notions of the relationship between 'The West' as a moral and racial category and the performance of structures of gender were to form a new space for gendered power relations in Xiamen.

Patriarchal discourses on ideal femininities were related to the perceived traits of Chinese women – passive, submissive and supportive. The Western woman was hence constructed to represent what was described by an interviewee as a 'third gender' (26, Australia) who took on traditionally masculine traits such as aggressiveness, assertiveness and forcefulness. Western women described the experience of being away from the sexual gaze of both Western men and Chinese men and were undergoing a process of de-sexualization where they described themselves as needing emotional skills such as self-confidence to 'survive' (42, Australia). Corporate wives were also renegotiating their gender roles and found themselves free from domestic duties and interpreting cultural illegibility on a day-to-day basis.

Western femininity was being transformed and reconsidered by both Western men and Western women in Xiamen. Extreme versions of patriarchal power relationships inherent in gender discourse in the West were in some cases being reaffirmed by men and resisted by women. In this case, Western women were constructed as the Other as opposed to the Chinese woman who was seen by many Western men as representative of a femininity which had been lost to modern 'assertive' Western women.

Western women also took on an identifiably new power role. To Western men, she tended to represent the gender expectations and value structure of 'home'. Her presence recalled the moral implications of a world imbued with discourses of equality, rights and status. For example, Gail from the United States explained her experience of being perceived as a representative of the 'morality of home':

> Married or not married, wife or no wife here – they all have Chinese girlfriends. We look around at all these Western guys – losers in their own countries – and they have all got these beautiful women. And no way would these people even look at them in their home country. It's a whole different lifestyle... The ego of the men – it's just unbelievable! Suddenly they are saying 'oh this girl loves me!' Yeah right! Yeah right she does! She sees dollar signs, she sees a way out, she sees a green card. She doesn't love you, loser. They know that we know that they are losers. We know them too well. We know exactly what's going on and exactly what they are thinking. And they know we're right.

This expression that 'they know that we know' was recognition of a form of disciplinary power that many Western women in Xiamen recounted as a feeling they held over Western men. The disciplinary gaze of the moral order of home was held by the Western woman, who, in this altered relationship of power, seemed to hold a form of authority over what was acceptable or not 'at home'. White femininity in this sense resisted but also supported both racialized and gendered power structures. In this sense, white women constitute the 'guardians of white moral authority and civilization through the control of white masculine excess' (Hunter, Swan and Grimes: 415). This function of white women as protectors and reproducers of civilization (Byrne 2006) existed in the physical embodiment and 'gaze' of white woman as representative of 'home'. The Western woman hence functioned as the physical presence of a cultural reminder and exercised embodied disciplinary power over the actions of Western men. Rhonda from Australia explained this further:

> Sometimes you feel like you're imposing on them when you walk into a bar and they are all there with their girlfriends. It's like, just because you're a *laowai* and you're a woman you are going to tell them off or something.

Women from Western countries were dealing with multiple shifts in power and contradictory gendered discourse. While they recounted being treated like 'one of the boys' (26, Australia) they also recounted feeling as if they are the 'eyes of home' (Field diary, 12 August 2005).

Men also experienced contradictory shifts in gendered discourse. While Chinese women were constructed as a version of a passive hyper-femininity which reaffirmed the Western male position at the perceived top of a gendered and racialized hierarchy, the women from 'home' were seen as opposing this power relationship. Western women represented a morality which placed them at a perceived lower position of gendered authority.

These contrasting and contradicting constructions of Western women as both representatives of Western morality and as threatening to white hegemonic patriarchy in Xiamen was evidence of global mobility creating spaces that allow both resistance to and reaffirmation of historicized gendered and racialized power relationships. It was only through experiencing and encountering the emotional structures of anxiety, ecstasy and fear that the taken-for-granted power structures of home were bought into question. The result was a process of interpretation of difference which took the form of Appiah's (2006) value 'conversation'.

The repositioning of self within the moral landscape was also a gendered and racialized practice.

The result of this repositioning of self was the creation of often contradictory notions of gendered relationships which, at its extremes, saw Western men seeking patriarchal affirmation and women acting as resisters to these same patriarchal values. The 'Other' (Chinese) woman functioned both as a disruption to the moral order of home and the embodiment of a femininity which affirmed patriarchal and Western dominance. The experience of structures of vulnerability at the day-to-day level led to a reconstitution of power which was often complex and contradictory and demonstrates the continuing relevance of historicized context and thick social structure for those living global lives.

Conclusion

The re-emergence of structure and community in Xiamen is closely tied to the ways gendered and racialized discourse are constructed at the local level. The experience of vulnerability led to the possibility of reconsidered power relations through processes of the 'genderization of race' and the 'racialization of gender'. At its extremes, Western men constructed Chinese women as representative of a passive hyper-femininity and Chinese men as representatives of an immoral 'Other' masculinity which reaffirmed a Western male position at the top of both a perceived gendered and racialized hierarchy.

It must be noted that I have deliberately used examples of the extremes of experiences of the construction of gendered and racialized power dynamics. These examples served to demonstrate that the vulnerabilities of global mobility allowed for the creation of spaces which at once recreated and contested multiple shared meanings and shaped the way that people interpret the environment around them.

The examples suggest that the gendered and racial constructions of the colonial era continue to be alive and relevant within the global era. This supports feminist writings that argue for an emphasis on the social contexts under which agents reflect, deliberate and cooperate with each other (Brooks and Wee 2008: 510). It is within the historical and cultural context that situated agents consider and criticize their social conditions while articulating new interpretations of them (Brooks and Wee 2008: 509). Postcoloniality exists and is performed together with globality and understanding this complex and often contradictory relationship is fundamental to understanding contemporary forms of migration.

Gender and race were 'geographies of power' (Mahler and Pessar 2006: 42) which were situated within historical context and formed links between colonial and contemporary discourses of 'East' and 'West'. At the same time, global mobility and the processes of vulnerability provided the context for the creation of new spaces for the questioning and contestation of these same technologies of power. This affirms the hypothesis of Willis and Yeoh (2002: 554), who argue that 'a consideration of gender dimensions of transnationalism among elites is clearly one area where challenges to hegemonic processes through transnational practices, in this case patriarchal norms, may be evident'. The processes of vulnerability and the subsequent reconsideration of gendered and racialized discourse show that indeed global mobility does provide spaces for such challenges to hegemonic gender practices. At the same time, however, the vulnerabilities of global mobilities also create the conditions for reaffirmation of these hegemonic practices. The multiple contradictory meanings that result create an environment where historically contextualized hegemonic discourses may come in contact with resistance, change and dynamism.

Such dynamism is created through local interpretation and emotional action. Discourses on social structure such as gender and race are both contested *and* recreated in relation to place and emotional structures. Rather than place, structure and emotion disappearing from meaningful social purview in the context of globalization, in fact the interpretation of place and the experience of emotional structures are central to the ongoing maintenance and reconfiguration of gendered and racialized power relationships.

7
Home

It was the processes of vulnerability and interpretation that created the conditions for the privileged migrants in Xiamen to reconsider notions of 'home'. 'Home' is conceptualized here as a multi-tiered and flexible category which refers not only to the city or region one belongs to but also to a wider notion of national belonging, and wider still, to a notion of being from 'The West'. The notion of 'home', and the levels of abstraction it encompasses, functions as a moral category which holds a regulatory function, in the sense that it represents familiar structures and moral order. This regulatory nature of 'home' is reconsidered and re-engaged with at the same time that the concept of 'home' is constructed and imagined. In this way, the interpretive processes of repositioning the self within a moral landscape are productive of social structures *and* are an element of structural articulation.

Just as it is imperative to emphasize the historical context of categories of gender and race, likewise the role of journeys and the notion of home in the history of the modern Western consciousness are valid today. The nation state as an imagined community (Anderson, B. 1991) is linked to the experience and construction of nostalgia as a communal construction of moral categories of the West, nation and self. Privileged Western migrants in Xiamen can be seen as modern Simmelian strangers who function to both maintain and dissolve national stereotypes and to question the values linked to these notions of home.

Strangers and stereotypes

It had been an average working day in Xiamen when Hans gets in the taxi waiting for him at exactly 4.45 pm to take him back to his apartment near the centre of the city. The humidity is stifling and he winds down the taxi window and lights a cigarette, feeling the city and its smells and sounds on his skin. Hans settles in for a 20-minute ride through chaos when the taxi suddenly slows down and the driver shouts 'laowai!' [foreigner!] and frantically points at two blonde-haired people walking on the side of the road. Hans has never seen them before but the taxi driver seems to assume they are friends due to their common status as foreign. The pair notices the taxi and the embarrassed Hans in the back seat and walk over to the open window. 'Hi!' says Hans 'Need a ride?' 'No thank you, we are just exploring. Where are you from?' 'Germany', replies Hans and returns the question. 'We are from France' they say. 'Well, better go. Nice to have met you. Perhaps see you around'. The taxi crunches into gear and makes it through the orange traffic light, just in time.

The only information that the people in this setting had was each other's status as insiders and outsiders in this particular place and at other particular places. Hans and the French couple were foreign, and shared a bond as outsiders in Xiamen and from the Chinese taxi driver. The taxi driver in this scenario was an 'invisible Other' who did not participate in the conversation, except to acknowledge and reinforce the shared status of the *laowai* as Western. This bond was expressed in Hans' willingness to immediately offer to share his taxi. The only other piece of information which was gathered about the three foreigners was their connection to a nation state. From this fleeting, urban encounter, identity priorities have been set and assumptions would then likely be made about cultural background, beliefs and values of these strangers. From a brief interaction, judgements and connections can be made with others who may or may not inhabit Hans' social world again.

The image of strangers has always played a key role in capturing the dynamic of modernity and the division of 'here' and 'there'. Simmel's ([1900] 1978) metropolitan social actors experienced a sense of objectification in a setting where they were considered outsiders or as representative of the remote. As a result, strangers – the objects of this remoteness – were not treated as individuals but as abstractions of a certain type. Strangers become someone who may have very broad or specific commonalities or non-commonalities. Simmel ([1907] 1978: 406) says:

> In the case of a person who is a stranger to the country, the city, the race, etc., however, this non-common element is once more nothing individual, but merely a strangeness of origin, which is or could be common to many strangers. For this reason, strangers are not really conceived as individuals, but as strangers of a particular type: the

element of distance is no less general in regard to them than the element of nearness.

The distance or nearness between the self and the stranger was something that was interpreted and negotiated during interaction. Geographical and cultural 'home' (whether in terms of region, nation or 'The West') and the general abstractions it entailed were an important marker for such stranger encounters.

David from the United Kingdom described the assumptions made about strangers in Xiamen based on national 'home':

> Of course I am aware of nationality. I'm aware that this person is from this country and that person is from that country. I ask people when I meet them where they come from. It's just one of those questions, and it's an important question – not just for the person asking but for the person answering. We all want to know where everybody came from. I know it's not necessary, but as long as there are nation-states, it is an important part of what a person is and who a person is. Because, whether we like it or not we all have our own cultural baggage and part of that baggage is our nationality. For example, it's almost like saying, what's your name? When people first start travelling its one of the most common questions to ask, and it's because it's something we've become used to. Another question is what do you do? Or how long have you been here? If you asked anybody who are you or what are you, which are very fundamental questions, they will say their name and their nationality.

David, a long-term Xiamener, was aware that nationality played an important part in identifying the self and others and their relationships. All those I interviewed expressed a heightened awareness, once in a community of strangers such as Xiamen, that their nationality was attached to assumptions about character and values and led to either belonging or not belonging to particular social groups. Often, this awareness of the centrality of nationality in stranger interactions was spoken about in terms of being faced with stereotypes.

Raban (1974) applied Simmel's theory to contemporary multi-cultural urban settings where he argued fleeting encounters with others were the norm. He noted that in a fast-paced community of strangers, we need a quick easy-to-use set of stereotypes, or 'cartoon outlines', with which to classify the people we encounter. According to both Simmel and Raban, this contrasts with previous eras or village life where most of the people dealt with are known (or are someone in your family circle) and share an established relationship through systems of kinship, place and shared history (Raban 1974; Simmel [1907] 1978). This gave modern urban strangers an existence where they were objectified as a part of an abstract 'cartoon outline' from which others draw assumptions based on their own subjective, historical and cultural understandings of identity markers such as nationality. For Xiameners, life in a multi-national setting meant being confronted with such national stereotypes to a larger degree than they had been at 'home'.

Scott from England described being objectified as a part of a stereotype by a Chinese person:

> Yesterday I was walking through an area and a couple of Chinese walked past me and said '*meiguoren*! [American]' You know. In fact, I called back to them in Chinese 'no! I'm English!' This stereotype is extremely strong here. It's strong, even when the people know you well. They still have difficulty breaking the perception of us...I get angry.

Being objectified falsely led Scott to experience anger. He was angry at being referred to as American instead of English, a result of drawing on his own understandings of stereotypes. The processes of objectification seemed to involve both stereotyping and being stereotyped according to nationality. Scott's anger was an emotional response to this urban stereotyping scenario. His anger created a situation where his nationality was at the forefront of identity and created a space for him to consider what it is that separates him from people from the United States and what he considers makes him essentially British. In such instances, national identity and connections with homelands were perceived to be under threat (Fechter 2007: 117). This led nationality to become a more important indicator of who a person was and how they were seen by others and saw others now than before leaving home.

It was in the negotiation and articulation of the meanings of these stereotypes that the participants were engaging in a process of repositioning themselves within the moral landscape of home. Stephen from the United States said: 'We spend a lot of time breaking down stereotypes. Giving substance to people.' The breaking down of stereotypes was part of the process of repositioning the self within the moral landscape and had two contrasting social effects. First, this repositioning led to the maintenance and reaffirmation of home and nation through performances and articulation of home-based identities. Second, this process contributed to the questioning of national values and structures and the questioning of the meaning of 'home'.

As a result, home was renegotiated as the manifestation of a moral landscape which was constantly reconstructed and negotiated in relation to vulnerability and difference at the level of the local and the particular. This process allowed for both the reaffirmation and the contestation of the moral landscape of 'home'. I begin by describing the reaffirmation of national stereotypes through nostalgic performance.

Remembering home: Performing nostalgia

Tony agreed to supply the face-paint for the rugby union final between Australia and England being shown at the pub. He'd managed to find a costume shop in an alley-way near Zhong Shan Street and arrived at the pub half-an-hour before kick-off. The pub is already buzzing with people ordering beer and food. Fish-and-chips comes wrapped, traditional English style, in newspaper and it doesn't seem to matter that rather than The Sun, grease stains were on a Chinese Communist party-run newspaper. Tony's girlfriend, Hong Li, is busy painting red-and-white St George's crosses on faces and looks confused when Joe from Sydney demands she open the box of green and gold instead. As the national anthems begin, the painted faces stand, raising their VBs and Newcastle Browns to the television screen, hands on hearts.

Such performances of national identity and belonging were done together with others who were perhaps outsiders in terms of nationality, but also insiders – Westerners. The above scenario would doubtlessly have included many Americans and Europeans who were joining the festivities, regardless of their lack of specific cultural familiarity with the rugby event. The urban environment of Xiamen was created as the 'Other' in such a setting. The rugby festivities were a celebration not just of belonging to a specific nation but of belonging to a wider notion of 'Western-ness' which separated 'us' from the differences of 'them' – the China outside the walls of the pub. This shared collective imagination of being 'Western' was also being performed here, alongside national heritage.

It has been noted that strangers in Xiamen became national beings to a larger extent than they ever were at home. At home, those around them were assumed to share, to some degree or other, similar cultural heritage and similar understandings of place, values and world view. Away from home, attachment to a nation became one of Raban's (1974) 'cartoon outlines' which resulted not only in an awareness of national stereotypes but the production and performance of nostalgic memory.

The awareness of difference resulted in a concurrent awareness of what constituted familiarity and, in some instances, the performance of memory and heightened articulation of national bonds (see also Clarke 2005; Hindman 2008; Walsh 2007).

Nostalgia here refers to the communal construction of memories of home (whether the West or the nation). Nostalgia was the practice of the construction of home as a site of ideal moral order which existed in contrast to its 'Other' – Xiamen. The nostalgic home lay in the past and the perhaps distant future. In the present place (Xiamen), such nostalgia was performed in the form of heightened national identity as the meanings of home were reconsidered in relation to difference.

Jack, a 28-year-old New Zealander, described this nostalgic construction of 'home':

> The number of times you've seen people singing 'I come from the land down-under' here, you know? They wouldn't do that back home. But when you are away there are all the heightened things about your home.

Jack's description of this banal nationalism (Billig 1995) resonates with the experience of ecstatic liminality. It was while away from the perceived structures of home that nationality was heightened and performed in ways that 'they wouldn't do back home'.

Nostalgic performances of nationality were often recounted as being related to a sense of liminal behaviour that would not have happened 'at home'. Josie, from Australia, described her experience of Australia Day in Xiamen as engaging in activity with others that she would have avoided had she been in Australia:

> My friend Phoebe and I discovered it was ANZAC day – we only found out because I went online and saw it was. We said oh my god! Its Anzac day! We contacted everyone we knew and said you have to come to Tian Lai bar! We told them it's a big part of our national thing! It's important to us! We are going to be playing Two Up! We got there and we realized neither of us knew how to play. Both of us had printed instructions but we both expected the other person to know. I thought, she's Aussie, she'll know and she thought the same about me! After she'd had a few drinks she got up on her chair and gave a speech that she'd prepared about Aussie soldiers at war. It was very embarrassing and there's no way she would have done that at home. Then we went to the bathrooms to compare our printouts. There were

lots of Westerners there. We ended up trying to teach these people how to play Two-Up because they'd all come along to learn it and we didn't want them to know that we didn't know what we were doing. When I left, there was a bunch of Canadians and Poms sitting around still playing – they were so into it! They loved it!

Josie and her friend's organization of Australia Day festivities happened only because they were away from Australia. Neither had ever played the traditional gambling game associated with Australia's national day before; yet in Xiamen, they felt confident to teach other Westerners about their culture and its history.

At a national level, nostalgic performance is also experienced by non-Western migrants such as Kong's (1999) Singaporean transmigrants in China who asserted their 'Singaporeanness' in ways they would not have in Singapore through the use of invented traditions and the creation of a 'little Singapore' area in Beijing. In Xiamen, the ANZAC day event described above was attended by other Westerners rather than the local Chinese population and was a performance of both a shared national identity and a wider sense of belonging to a community defined by being 'Western'.

The nostalgic 'home' was likewise consumed in the form of products that held a new value in Xiamen. For example, an entry from my field notes describes the commodification and performance of national identity in response to vulnerability:

> Rhonda and Jerry have spent a lot importing a barbeque from Brisbane. It took them ages to get approval for it and get it through customs but it arrived last week and tonight they had a celebration barbie at their place. They seem to have found a great butcher here and had 'real' steak and salad the way we do at home. Within minutes the men had assembled around the barbie while the women huddled around the kitchen counter gossiping and chopping vegies. It was strange being on their tiny balcony with a huge BBQ and a glass of sav blanc and looking down on the rickshaws and peddlers on the street below. Somehow this ritual of home meant more, or different because of that street below.
>
> (Field diary entry, 16 May 2005)

Home was an imaginary and was located in the past. This 'home' was remembered through such communal performance. Products such as the barbeque (a type which was unavailable in Xiamen and was specially imported), the steak and the wine held a social value within this group which was related to a shared memory of 'home'. In this field-diary entry, I was aware that this consumption and performance of nostalgia was relevant because of its contrast to difference in the 'street below'. The present place of difference (Xiamen) was contrasted against a realm of familiarity (Rhonda and Jerry's house). Said (2001: 186) described the construction of memory of home as the linking of the past with the present:

> Habits of life, expression, or activity in the new environment inevitably occur against the memory of these things in another environment. Thus, both the new and the old environments are vivid, actual, occurring together contrapuntally ... There is also a particular sense of achievement in acting as if one were at home wherever one happens to be.

Rhonda and Jerry felt this sense of achievement in creating this zone of nostalgia. Hindman (2008) describes how expatriates in Kathmandu use nationally appropriate consumption to create the residential home as a hyper-nationalized space. She suggests this is a means to deal with fear and insecurity by insulating themselves in stereotyped spaces. In this way, the house represents and becomes 'home' in a broader national and 'Western' sense (Hatfield 2010). I argue that this bringing the past ('home') into the present (Xiamen) was a communal means of interpreting difference and was an effect of the structures of vulnerability. In this way, the domestic home space is seen to not exist prior to identities and relations but is their integral part (Massey 2005: 10).

Xiameners were examples of Clifford's (1992) notion of 'dwelling-in-travelling'. For Clifford, cultures exist as sites of both dwelling and travelling and the everyday practices of consuming home while allowing migrants to create moments of both movement and stasis and difference and familiarity (Clarke 2005). Urry (2000) continues this point and argues that people dwell in and through being both at home and away, through the dialectic of roots and routes (see also Nowicka 2007).

A further example of this roots/routes dialectic and the social nature of home as both remembering and becoming is through the communal performance of humour. Many interviewees, when asked what they miss about home, said they missed the sense of humour. For example, as Alan from England described it:

> I miss certain things that only foreigners can give me. Particularly say, English, or Commonwealth ... Australians, British, New

Zealanders – people coming from a strong English background. What I miss more than anything is humour. Humour doesn't transgress cultures as diverse as England and China. I find Germans, strangely enough, have a humour not too far different from England. Americans are a little bit stranger. I recall one evening, being in a bar, it must have been in 1997, and I heard some people speaking my local dialect – I'm from the north-east of England, a Geordie – and I heard two Geordies talking and I went to join them and I spent the next hour or two laughing because they not only had my Engiish sense of humour, but they also had our regional sense of humour. It was so uplifting for me because I hadn't had it for a couple of years. I missed it. When people ask me 'What do you miss most?' that's always my answer – humour.

Humour was described by Alan as a culturally specific mode of interaction and, in Xiamen, 'home' was constructed as a site where this interaction made sense and was understood. The more one shared a geographical history (nation, region, city, suburb), the more this mode of communication allowed for this history to be performed in humour. In this way, humour provided a social mechanism for remembering and constructing 'home' as a place with meaning and familiarity.

Vulnerability was at times described as being 'reigned in' or 'stabilized' through this communal form of nostalgia. David from England described how a comedy television programme from home was a way of 'remembering' home which he found 'grounding':

You feel more isolated here. Perhaps that's why I spend a lot of time with other Westerners, to nurture that isolated feeling that might creep up on you when you're here…I can go a week without seeing another foreign face…Westerners help me keep my head together and remind me of my roots. Like meeting up with Simon and watching Monty Python or some other comedy show. It's a really good way of remembering.

In this quote, David was suggesting that the difference and cultural isolation he faced in Xiamen needed to be counteracted with familiarity in order to maintain his own sense of self and identity. By sharing a comedy programme with a fellow Englishman, David was provided with a form of protection against the uncertainties of vulnerability and allowed him to remember his 'roots' in another place and time. In this way, the notion of 'home' as it was performed and consumed in Xiamen functioned as a regulatory mechanism to counteract the processes of vulnerability (Hindman 2008).

Further, David's quote serves to highlight how 'home' existed as an *ideal* site of moral order. We have seen how the decision to initially leave home was often made as a result of tensions between the value of individualism and the expectations of the communal. Many participants felt they didn't belong at home, or were on the 'fringes' before they left for Xiamen. The communal performance of home such as sharing humour and nationalistic rituals functioned to produce 'home' as a site of ideal moral familiarity and forms of belonging that nevertheless held a regulatory role.

The nostalgic performance of national identity as a result of global mobility resulted in the communal articulation of 'home'. Occurring concurrently, however, was the questioning of these communal bonds and the structures of home. With national identity in the foreground, Xiameners were in a position to ask about their own relationship to the moral landscape of home and the values that existed in that different time and place. It was here, in both the nostalgic performance and questioning of home, that the values associated with both the 'West' and the nation continued to be both reaffirmed and contested.

Deconstructing home

Faced with cultural difference and 'illegibility', Xiameners found various social means to interpret and understand difference. Vulnerability allowed for a conversation between the self and wider values that underpin global mobility. The awareness of difference led to an ongoing conversation about values of home in the West and in a particular nation state.

Xiameners found themselves defining their identity in newly emphasized national terms and became aware of the assumptions made about them by others on the basis of their belonging to a particular nation. Reflecting on these stereotypes became a process of renegotiation between the self and wider values associated with being in a specific place. For example, Emile from France explained:

> You have a lot of things that people say French people are. They are like this, or they are like that. I tend to more and more see what they mean. I was so proud of it when I was in France. There is a cliché though that French people are arrogant. That's very true. Arrogant.

I agree with that. It wasn't so clear when I was in France. I couldn't really define it. But now I can really see what people mean.

It was only in an environment of cultural distance and difference that Emile was able to reflect on the values and traits of his home. Many respondents spoke of possessing a new 'objective' stance on their homeland since arriving in Xiamen. Stephen from the United States said:

Living here has made me able to look at things from the outside. The objective point of view I suppose, even though I am American. In that way, yeah, it's a good chance to see how the rest of the world sees America... Many Americans fit the stereotype other people seem to have of them. But many of them don't.

This 'outside' view of home often resulted in home itself being objectified and reconsidered. Vulnerability allowed Xiameners to ask: Why are things done differently here? Why do other nationalities think differently to me? How *do* things work at home? Frederik from the Netherlands remarked to me that 'It's almost like you learn more about your home when you are here than you do about China'. This dialogue between self, difference and familiarity led to both a reaffirmation of *and* resistance to the moral landscape of home.

Xiameners were engaged in a constant process of comparing or relating the self to multiple others. Bashkow (2006: 240) also described this moral functioning of ordering of home and the universe in terms of 'us' and 'them':

These pan-human discourses of otherness serve an important moral function in providing an evaluative meta-commentary on aspects of the self that the other casts into relief: a ready framework for exploring alternatives to one's own culture's conventional morality.

The interviewees were part of such an 'evaluative meta-commentary' and the 'illegible' space of Xiamen allowed for this framework of reconsidering the common sense of home. For example, when Jess from England arrived in China, she became aware of the micro-rules of etiquette governing her cultural self and recognized contradictions with her wider sense of the values she associated with 'home':

You see the differences. I mean, everything's so serious in England. Things like table manners and there are rules about what you should do. But then again, thinking about it, they've [the Chinese] all got a lot of expectations on them and we never had that. We have a lot more freedom in that way. It's like how gay people are not allowed here and we have so many gay people in England. So I guess we have more freedom in that way, but then again you have to sit up properly at dinner!

Likewise, Gail from New York started to question the values of her homeland when faced with vulnerability in Xiamen:

I watch the people here … We are law crazy in the United States and we'll sue you for anything and here I see babies riding on bicycles or on the back of a motor-bike just nonchalantly – one or two year olds. And no railings anywhere! I climb mountains here and there are no railings. If you take the wrong step – you're gone. I always say OHS and health inspectors would close China down entirely. We have so many laws in America and every law is broken here. Yet we survive here. We get along. We somehow manage. So I think – why do we have so many laws at home? Since I've been here, sometimes I start thinking we go overboard at home.

Gail's conversation between difference, vulnerability and home was continual while living in China. It was as she learned about China and interpreted difference that this conversation became possible. Home was at once performed and remembered nostalgically, but at the same time seen 'objectively' and critiqued in the presence of the 'Other'.

Bill, who had been in China for more than 15 years at the time of the interview, continued to produce and critique home as a site of negotiation between difference and familiarity:

When you see the way young people respect you here – they stand up for you on the bus. Not just for me but for older Chinese people. They have respect for old people, and that's not there at home.

Such comparisons between home and Xiamen were often spoken about in terms of the differences in perceived values associated with 'doing business' in China. In making comparisons, similarities sometimes became evident which challenged traditional notions of the Asian 'Other' and the 'West'. Sally explained:

I've been thinking, what is the difference between foreigners and Chinese people, and I think when it comes down to doing business, at the heart of it, it's really the same. It really is who you know and what connections you have with people. But here it's not overt. As in, at home you get to formalize it but that's not how it starts out. Here it starts with a connection and it depends on how good that person's contact is and then you eventually get down to it…because that's how our culture is, we formalize things. It just depends on how good that person's connection is. They [the Chinese] are more into doing more of the informal stuff and never get around to the formal stuff like you would in Europe or Australia. But we do still work with the idea that it is who you know and the connections you make.

In comparing the cultural self and the cultural 'Other', Sally was placing herself within a wider moral landscape. In interpreting differences, she was also interpreting similarities and could reflect on and construct the meanings of the values of home and values here. In this way, the meanings and values of home were contested and reconstructed here in Xiamen, yet they held their value there, at home.

The nostalgic practices of remembering and questioning home can only be done at a distance, in relationship to difference. The result of this relationship between vulnerability and nostalgia is that the home one leaves is never the same as the home to which one returns.

Nostalgia and deferring home

Through the interpretation of difference, 'home' became the site of nostalgic remembrance which allowed for not only the heightened awareness and performances of national identity but also the questioning of the previously taken-for-granted structures of home. This dynamic dialogue between vulnerability and nostalgia resulted in a version of home which functioned as the manifestation of both a reaffirmation and resistance to the structures and values of the West. In this relationship to difference, home is continually produced and reproduced rather than existing as a static site which remains unchanged and unchallenged.

The home that existed in the nostalgic present for those in Xiamen tended to shift from the experience of home in the past. While home existed in the past and perhaps in the future, it was constructed and performed 'here', in Xiamen, in the present. This shifting notion of home was demonstrated through interview narratives which recounted returning home as a disappointment. For Benson and O'Reilly's (2009a:

610) lifestyle migrants, home was also romanticized and retrospective stories were found not to reflect objective reality. Most Westerners I interviewed spoke about the return home as failing to match expectations. For example, Alan from England described his experience of returning home:

> You might find this a bit strange but when I first got here in '95 I didn't leave the Chinese mainland for three years. At almost the end of three years I jumped on a plane and went to Sydney, Australia, where my two daughters are living now. I remember my oldest daughter saying 'you know, Dad, it took you more than a week when you arrived in Sydney to adjust. You were so spaced out. You were so shocked'. You leave and then you get home and nobody is paying you any damned attention at all! Nobody looks at me in Australia and that took a bit of adjusting too.

When Alan returned to the West, he was aware that at 'home' he was no longer an outsider who was different to the local environment. He felt 'shocked' and 'needed to adjust' *because* he was in a place of familiarity.

Others spoke about the return home as a realization that the experience of vulnerability and difference has led to personal change. Kathy, for example, felt on the outside once home:

> As a foreigner that's been here long term, I don't realize it when I am with all the other foreigners that have been here long term. Its only when you leave. Always doing numbers in your head. You see an opportunity and you go 'we could do this'. And everyone else at home is looking at you weird and going oh god. It's too intense for them.

Once Kathy returned home, it was those at home who she saw as 'different' to herself. She then began the processes of vulnerability again, interpreting difference this time 'at home' in relation to her experience in Xiamen. Likewise, Stephen from the United States described the experience of being a 'double-outsider' – both at home and in Xiamen – which he said led him to exist in an almost third zone of space:

> People at home can't understand the way we live here. The same as the Chinese people can't understand the way we live. Everybody is getting up and going to work in the morning, trying to make a living, trying to find a person to like, trying to get a relationship. It's basic.

> But the way we do it is different. I think the way is far too different to understand.

Stephen's experiences of returning home led him to experience difference *there*, and, as a consequence, he felt on the outside at home ('People at home can't understand the way we live here') *and* in Xiamen ('The same as the Chinese people can't understand the way we live'). He suggested that the Chinese people and the people at home shared experiences in common ('Everybody is getting up and going to work in the morning, trying to make a living, trying to find a person to like, trying to get a relationship'), but that he sat outside of both these groups. He shared this experience of being faced with difference on two fronts with others like him in Xiamen ('But the way *we* do it is different'). For Stephen, the vulnerable processes that he experienced through the emotional structures of anxiety, ecstasy and fear transformed him and led him to no longer feel an insider at 'home'. He existed in a constant state of being between 'here' and 'there' and suggested that this was unlikely to come to a defined end point ('I think the way is far too different to understand').

We have seen how the decision to initially leave home is made in a context of anxiety. This anxiety was defined as a tension between the value of individualism and the perceived contrasting expectations of the communal. Many of those I spoke to felt an 'outsider' at home, before they left for Xiamen. This anomic tension between individualism and the community, however, is not rectified upon return. Instead, the Xiameners felt a deeper sense of being on the outside when they returned which often fuelled their ongoing global mobility. Mobility, therefore, both challenges and recreates the notion of home (Nowicka 2007).

I have used the concept of liminality to discuss the journey from the West as a rite-of-passage. The Xiameners were described as experiencing liminality on two fronts – they felt they didn't need to comply with the rules and norms of home nor China. In an anthropological sense, a rite-of-passage should come to an end with the return to the point of origin as a changed person, with higher status in the community (Turner 1969). This notion of 'home' as a stable moral anchor can be seen as entrenched within the Western literary canon. Homer's *Odysseus* was perhaps the first portrayal of this narrative of the traveller who was marred by the immoral and dangerous difference of the 'East' yet returned home an improved man, and in doing so reaffirmed the values of property, family and continuing life (Powell 2004: 158).

This journeying narrative can be found throughout modern Western literature, arts and film whereby a transformative journey leads the protagonist back to their original starting point having learned a new appreciation for the values of home (see Graziosi and Greenwood 2007). Such cyclical journeys away from home, and back towards it, serve to construct home as a fixed point of moral order and fixity.

This notion of a stable and constant home is mirrored in the work of Said (2001) who, in his discussions on the exilic condition, remained relatively unreflective about home. Ling (2007), however, claims that Said's treatment of exile does reveal certain assumptions about the nature of home. For Said, home means being settled and exists within fixed, familiar territory. Said's home is 'now and forever' and is memorialized through exile. Home therefore becomes 'set, over-determined and eternalized' (Ling 2007: 136). From this perspective, power and knowledge remain located within this eternal and stable home and exemplify the 'conventional' and the 'habitual'. The exile's journey is away from and towards an eventual and desired return to this place of fixity, certainty and consensus.

For most of the participants in this research, such a return to a stable, constant home was impossible. These journeys of vulnerability and the nostalgic construction and critique of home that resulted failed to reach a fixed, stable end point. Callum, from Scotland, described his experience of returning home and not belonging in the place he had imagined from a distance while in Xiamen:

> In Australia you get the tall poppy syndrome. It's an export from Scotland. It's worse in Scotland. You're not allowed to say you're successful. If you do, you're an arse... When I went home not long ago I ran into a guy I had worked with. I'd known him for years. I had gone out and ran into him and hadn't seen him for years and years. He said 'how's it going?' I said, 'aye, not bad'. I asked him where he is now and he said he was at a factory in Livingstone. I told him I was living in China and the mood just changed. He says to his pal, 'Get this, I ask him how he's getting on and he says aye, alright, I'm living in China'. And he didn't speak to me again. Literally refused to look at me.

The conversation between difference and home continued upon arrival back home. Callum was still questioning the values of home and his place within a wider moral landscape, even after arrival back home. The negotiation of home did not, therefore, end with the return.

Most interviewees returned to China after returning home and many now spend their lives moving back and forth across the globe.

Callum and Stephen could be described as 'rootless' cosmopolitans in the sense that their mobility has led them to constantly feel 'on the outside' or disconnected from place. Such cosmopolitanism was constructed within value 'conversations' which were facilitated by the emotional structures of vulnerability. The rootless cosmopolitan indeed can be seen to exist in communities such as Xiamen, yet, when examined at the local level, can also provide evidence for the continuing relevance of emotion, place and structure for global lives. These journeys suggest that such 'rootlessness' forms one facet of a dynamic relationship between vulnerability and the recreation of social structure.

This holds resonance with the work of Bhaba (1994) who described the creative potential within transnational spaces where the flows of global workers are increasing, such as Xiamen. He described such places as 'boundary zones' and argued that in an increasingly connected world such borders and frontiers of place become the location of the construction and creation of culture, value systems and social identities. More recently, Yeoh and Willis (2005: 269) described these places as 'contact zones' where 'difference is constantly encountered and negotiated'. These spaces provide the terrain for elaborating strategies of selfhood and communal representation because of their location at the frontline of the articulation and interpretation of 'differences'. Bhaba (1994: 269) referred to transnational spaces and border zones as 'interstices' which are the site for engagements of cultural differences which may be either consensual or conflictual:

> They may confound our definitions of tradition and modernity; realign the customary boundary between the private and the public, high and low; and challenge the normative expectations of development and progress.

Further, he argued that by re-conceptualizing culture as a category of translation we might open up a range of questions which link the growing interdisciplinarity of studies of globalizing processes (Bhaba 1994: 269). I have referred to this 'category of translation' as the 'interpretation of difference' which is made possible through the vulnerable processes outlined in Part I. Returning home did not, however, result in the escape from Bhaba's (1994) 'interstices'. Instead, the interstices shifted upon return. The geographical space of home provided the context for the continuation of the interpretation of difference.

For Derrida (1976), the interpretive process is also a form of 'pushing aside'. The deconstructive process of interpreting difference and the subsequent recreation of meaning are constantly moving, indefinitely dispersed and indefinitely deferred. Derrida (1976: 403) claimed that meaning could only arise in the 'presence of an absence'. This continual relevant absence or *difference* is described by Derrida as the 'trace'. The trace is that which is different, that which is not there. Derrida argues that it is in the writing of traces that we can 'determine the meaning of things' (Powell 2006). In this vein, home can be seen to exist as a trace – a meaningful concept only when it is opposed to what it is not. For Derrida (1976), meaning is forever deferred or postponed through endless webs of interpretation. 'Home' functions in this manner, as a manifestation of what is 'not there'. As a consequence, there is a continual aspect of interpretation at play within the concept of 'home'. While Derrida (1978: 284) claimed that 'language bears within itself the necessity of its own critique', I suggest that the notion of 'home' bears within itself this same necessity.

Home has been described here as the manifestation of the processes of interpretation of difference. What it represents is the processes of comparison against what it is not, or the non-present. 'Home' functions to undo and deconstruct the social structures and values associated with it. In this way, home is found in difference.

Conclusion

The function of 'home' is as both a moral category and as a manifestation of the processes of interpretation. Xiameners were described as Simmelian strangers who were confronted with national stereotypes to a higher degree than they had been at home. The awareness of difference and of the structures of home led to the communal performance of 'home' through demonstrations of a nostalgic 'home' which served to reinforce or reaffirm the values associated with a region, a nation or a wider sense of the 'West'. However, a heightened awareness of nationality also led to the deconstruction of the structures and values of home. 'Home' served a regulatory function throughout the experience of vulnerability while it was both contested and reaffirmed.

Unlike a pilgrimage or rite-of-passage, the journey towards home never ended. Vulnerability and nostalgia push home and belonging to the edges. The concept of home therefore held within it the necessity of comparison with difference. Even upon return to the place known as home, these comparative processes didn't cease to function.

This does not, however, imply that home and place are meaningless concepts. Instead, as we have seen, they are the very location of the construction of values and selfhood and have the capacity to produce alternative and competing discourses of power and community in the context of globality. As Rundell (2004) argued, 'absolute strangers do not simply inhabit a nation-state: they create and participate in the cultural projects and politics that give it form'. Emotion and place are central to the continuing dynamism of both local and global social structures. The journeys that have been recounted here are journeys of selfhood and journeys of wider narratives of what it means to be from 'The West'. While these journeys continue indefinitely, the continuing meanings of place, emotion and structure can be found in the traces of home.

8
Conclusion

The journeys recounted here suggest that models of 'rootless cosmopolitanism' are part of a much larger and more complex story. While vulnerability and the weakening of social structures do occur as a part of global mobility, this vulnerability provides the conditions for the reconstruction of place-centred notions of power, structure and community. Further, the tracing of these journeys has described the centrality of global mobility for the production *and* contestation of wider-shared values that underpin Western globalism.

This provides support for Scheffler's (1999: 257) and Delanty's (2006: 27) argument that fluid cosmopolitanism allows 'newness' to enter the world. Such 'newness' continues to exist within historicized and contextualized social structures. The result of the processes of vulnerability was not the outright creation of new ideas about status, gender, race and nationality. Instead, vulnerability allowed for a complex 'conversation' to ensue with regard to these discursive boundaries, the result of which was not only the contestation of the taken-for-granted structures of home but also the recreation and reproduction of these same discursive boundaries. Migration, in this sense, is change at a quotidian level that can lead 'to further transformations in sending and receiving societies' (Portes 2010: 1551). This change potential within everyday migratory stories is deserving of continued attention in the social sciences.

This process of change began with the decision to leave home for Xiamen which was a result of the emotional structure of anxiety which was an expression of tensions between the value of individualism and the continued expectations of the communal.

Upon arrival in Xiamen the participants underwent a period of perceived freedom from both the social structural boundaries of 'home' and Xiamen. Faced with perceived cultural and linguistic difference, the participants were undergoing a process of liminality or the 'loosening of social structure' characterized by the emotional structure of anxiety.

The interaction with this perceived difference was understood through the emotional structure of fear. The vulnerable processes of anxiety, ecstasy and fear created the conditions which allowed for value 'conversations' (Appiah 2006) to occur as participants repositioned themselves within a moral landscape.

As the interpretation of difference ensued, divisions and connections were established with other Westerners in Xiamen. A hierarchy was established based on the length of time spend in China and knowledge of place, and gossip, secrets and trust were used as regulatory mechanisms as the participants re-engaged with community at the local level.

The repositioning of selves within moral landscapes was both a racialized and gendered practice. The vulnerabilities of global mobilities created the conditions for this reconsideration and renegotiation of gendered and racialized discourse and created spaces for both the continuation of historicized power relations and the creation of new, alternative identities.

Upon return home, this dialogue with difference did not cease. Instead, the location of difference shifted and, as such, home was continuously pushed to the edges. 'Home' existed therefore *within* the interpretative process. The notion of 'home' remained vital to the continuation of globally mobile life-paths and the consequent construction and contestation of the values that underpin this mobility (such as individualism, freedom and difference).

Historical discourses of 'home' as a stable site of moral order should be challenged. While 'home' is a constantly shifting 'trace' (Derrida 1978), this does not equate to evidence for a *condition* of free-floating cosmopolitanism. Rather, this supports the continued relevance of place, structure and emotion as linked and dynamic sites of both the creation and contestation of the values that underpin global mobility.

Cosmopolitanism should be conceptualized as transformative and processual, rather than a static 'condition'. This 'processual conception of the social' (Delanty 2006: 41) allows research such as this to further examine the location of the global within the local and to analyse the multiple and often contradictory ways that the social world is created out of encounters with difference. While Walsh (2006) argues that mobile identities are framed by 'simultaneous, interdependent notions of attachment and detachment' (p. 276), such identities are also framed by the localized daily negotiation of tensions between individualism and community, familiarity and difference and freedom and restraint.

Migration from the West and research agendas

There are four areas that future research in this field should consider. First, globalization research needs to take an inter-disciplinary perspective. A focus on emotion allows a micro-level approach to global lives, yet these experiences should also be considered within larger frameworks of meaning. A recent response to an increase in research in the social sciences on emotion has led to a recent increase in studies which consider the emotional life of migrants (Walsh 2012: 43). This emphasis should be also maintained within globalization research generally. Svasek and Skrbis (2007: 379) emphasize the importance of this and indicate that this necessarily calls for an interdisciplinary approach:

> It is important to push interdisciplinary engagement with emotions and globalisation and to be open to findings as varied as the social sciences, medical studies and philosophy. Research needs to take a multi-level approach, exploring emotions as discourses, practices and embodied experiences.

In other words, sociology will always benefit from being open to methodological approaches and findings from disciplines outside their own in order to fully account for the multiple contexts of globalization and for the everyday realities of the globalizing places we inhabit (Conradson and Latham 2005a).

Second, this research has followed people from the West in one location from a temporal perspective. That is, I began with discussing the context of leaving home and concluded with discussions of returning home. It must be remembered that this linear model forms a methodological tool for pulling apart commonalities and similarities within the interview narratives and that lives rarely follow a straight-forward linear path from home, through a time of liminality, re-engagement with community and then return home. Instead, these processes often overlap, repeat and exist concurrently with each other. The purpose of the linear model adopted here was to demonstrate that vulnerability or a loosening of social structure provided the conditions for a later re-engagement with social structure and community.

Further research should explore these conceptual 'stages' in more depth and in isolation from each other in order to more fully comprehend the contexts and experiences of global mobilities. In-depth research into the motivations for leaving home, for example, could provide further detail into the experience of anomic tension which may influence the decision to become global. In particular, the gendered and racialized constructions of global vulnerabilities deserve continued attention from social scientists.

Additionally, queer and alternative gendered and sexual identities were not addressed here and could provide an interesting avenue for further research into the complex and often contradictory constructions of identity and belonging within globally mobile communities. Queer theory has contributed to the de-naturalizing of hetero-normative assumptions in much analysis of migration, yet there continues to be an absence of studies of migration and hetereosexualities in their temporal and spatial contexts (Walsh, Shen and Willis 2008).

Third, the perspectives of Chinese local communities have not been addressed here. Instead, this research has focused exclusively on the creation of community and identity for those from the 'West' living in Xiamen. Further research needs to link the experiences and perceptions of cultural difference, liminality and community from the Chinese point of view in order to bring a multi-focal approach to the fore. Such an approach would take into account not only Western historicized power relations but also Chinese understandings of the 'West' and notions of postcoloniality and globality.

Finally, as global power following the global economic crises continues to shift and takes an arguably new form, this raises important issues about the potential futures of privileged and skilled migration from stagnating Western economies to the rapidly developing nations. The effects of the financial crisis have already had a 'discernable impact on international migration patterns, trends and policies worldwide' (Koser 2009: 6). Such shifts in migration require governments to 'prioritize migration issues in responding to the financial crisis', yet there still remains a shortage of empirical data on migrants and their experiences (Koser 2009: 1). A 'brain drain' of skilled workers from their homelands will potentially increase as a result of the continuing crisis and as expatriates change location or return home as a result of shifts in the global job market (Koser 2009: 12). This movement of skilled migration as a response to the global economic crisis has particular implications in the Chinese context. The *New York Times* reported in August 2009:

Shanghai and Beijing are becoming new lands of opportunity for recent American college graduates who face unemployment at home nearing the double digits at home. Even those with limited or no knowledge of Chinese are heeding the call. They are lured by China's surging economy, the lower cost of living and a chance to bypass some of the dues-paying that is common to first jobs in the United States.

(Seligson 2009)

Further research should monitor the experience of Western transnational workers during this time of restructuring of global economic power relations. This would necessarily involve examining the new status and new meanings attributed to white migrants in newly globalizing cities.

The journeys recounted of the Xiameners are transformative and as such they hold within them the potential for social change. The interaction between place, structure and emotion has shown that the globally mobile can be conceptualized as both forging reconsidered forms of identity and belonging as well as reconfirming continued historicized notions of these same social structures. Further, rather than 'rootless cosmopolitanism' existing as a condition of globality, it exists instead as one facet of the multiple ongoing journeys that continue to be embedded within forms of thick community and solidarity. As the numbers of middling Western migrants continue to increase, tracing such journeys and the meanings of home should be the focus of further empirical sociological enquiry.

Notes

2 Anxiety and Individualism

1. All names have been changed and every effort has been made to protect the anonymity of those who assisted with this research.

6 Gender and Race

1. The Xiamen Golf Society is currently inclusive of both women and Chinese male players.

References

Aalbers, M. 2009. 'Geographies of the financial crisis'. *Area*. Vol. 41 (1): 34–42.

Aguilar, F. 1999. 'Ritual passage and the reconstruction of selfhood in international labour migration'. *Sojourn: Journal of Social Issues in Southeast Asia*, January, Vol. 14(1): 98–139.

Ahmed, S. 2004. *The Cultural Politics of Emotion*. Edinburgh: Edinburgh University Press.

Albrow, M. and E. King, eds. 1990. *Globalization, Knowledge and Society*. London: Sage.

Albrow, M., Eade, J., Washbourne, N. and Durrschmidt, J. 1994. 'The impact of globalisation on sociological concepts: Community, culture and milieu'. *Innovation: The European Journal of Social Sciences*. Vol. 7 (4): 371–389.

Amit, V. 2007. 'Structures and dispositions of travel and movement'. In Amit, V. (ed.) *Going First Class? New Approaches to Privileged Travel and Movement*. Oxford: Berghahn Books.

Anderson, B. 1991. *Imagined Communities*. London: Verso.

Anderson, K. 1991. *Vancouver's Chinatown: Racial Discourse in Canada 1875–1980*. Montreal: McGill University Press.

Ang, I. 2000. 'Globalisation, "Asia" and the politics of space'. *Communal/Plural*. Vol. 8 (1): 5–7.

Appadurai, A. 1996. *Modernity at Large: Cultural Dimensions of Globalisation*. Minneapolis: University of Minnesota Press.

Appiah, K. 2006. *Cosmopolitanism: Ethics in a World of Strangers*. London: Penguin.

Archer, M. 2007. *Making Our Way Through the World: Human Reflexivity and Social Mobility*. Cambridge: Cambridge University Press.

Armbruster, H. 2010. 'Realising the self and developing the African': German immigrants in Namibia. *Journal of Ethnic and Migration Studies*. Vol. 36 (8): 1229–1246.

Barbalet, J. 1998. *Emotion, Social Theory and Social Structure: A Macrosociological Approach*. Cambridge: Cambridge University Press.

Bashkow, I. 2006. *The Meaning of Whitemen: Race, Modernity and the Orokaiva Cultural World*. Chicago: University of Chicago Press.

Bauman, Z. 1995. *Life in Fragments: Essays in Postmodern Morality*. Oxford: Blackwell.

Bauman, Z. 2000. *Liquid Modernity*. Cambridge: Polity.

Bauman, Z. 2006. *Liquid Fear*. Cambridge: Polity.

Bauman, Z. 2007. *Liquid Times: Living in an Age of Uncertainty*. Cambridge: Polity.

Beaverstock, J. 2002. 'Transnational elites in global cities: British expatriates in Singapore's financial district'. *Geoforum*. Vol. 33 (4): 525–538.

Beaverstock, J. 2011. 'Servicing British expatriate 'talent' in Singapore: Exploring ordinary transnationalism and the role of the 'expatriate' club'. *Journal of Ethnic and Migration Studies*. Vol. 37 (5): 709–728.

Beck, U. 1999. Living your own life in a runaway world: Individualism, globalisation and politics. In Hutton, W. and Giddens, A. (eds) *On the Edge: Living with Global Capitalism*, pp. 164–174. London: Vintage.

Beck, U. 2000. *The Brave New World of Work*. Cambridge: Polity.

Beck, U. 2006. *Cosmopolitan Vision*. Cambridge: Polity.

Benson, M. and O'Reilly, K. 2009a. Migration and the search for a better way of life: A critical exploration of lifestyle migration. *The Sociological Review*. Vol. 57 (4): 608–625.

Benson, M. and O'Reilly, K. 2009b. 'Lifestyle migration: Escaping to the good life?' In Benson, M. and O'Reilly, K. (eds) *Lifestyle Migration: Expectations, Aspirations and Experiences*. Farnham: Ashgate

Berman, M. 1983. *All That Is Solid Melts into Air: The Experience of Modernity*. London: Verso.

Bhaba, H. 1994. 'Frontlines/borderposts'. In Bammer, A. (ed.) *Displacements: Cultural Identities in Question*, pp. 269–272. Indianapolis: Indiana University Press.

Billig, M. 1995. *Banal Nationalism*. London: Sage.

Blakewell, O. 2010. 'Some reflections on structure and agency in migration theory'. *Journal of Ethnic and Migration Studies*. Vol. 36 (10): 1689–1708.

Bonnett, A. 1997. 'Geography, race and whiteness: Invisible traditions and current challenges'. *Area*. Vol. 29: 193–199.

Bonnett, A. 2004. *The Idea of the West: Culture, Politics and History*. Palgrave: Basingstoke.

Bonnett, A. 2008. 'White studies revisited'. *Ethnic and Racial Studies*. Vol. 31 (1): 185–196.

Brahm, L. 2004. *Doing Business in China the Sun Tzu Way*. Singapore: Tuttle Publishing.

Brooks, A. and Wee, L. 2008. 'Reflexivity and the transformation of gender identity: Reviewing the potential for change in a cosmopolitan city'. *Sociology*. Vol. 42 (3): 503–521.

Byrne, B. 2006. *White Lives: The Interplay of 'Race', Class and Gender in Everyday Life*. Routledge: New York.

Castles, S. 2010. 'Understanding global migration: A social transformation perspective'. *Journal of Ethnic and Migration Studies*. Vol. 36 (10): 1565–1586.

China Briefing. 2010. *Business Guide to China's Emerging Second and Third Tier Cities*. Dezan Shira and Associates: Hong Kong

Clancy-Smith, J. and Gouda, F. (eds) 1998. *Domesticating the Empire: Race, Gender and Family Life in French and Dutch Colonialism*. Charlottesville, VA: The University Press of Virginia.

Clarke, N. 2005. 'Detailing transnational lives of the middle: British working holiday makers in Australia'. *Journal of Ethnic and Migration Studies*. Vol. 31 (2): 307–322.

Clifford, J. 1992. 'Traveling cultures'. In Grossberg, L. (ed.) *Cultural Studies*. London: Routledge

Cohen, E. 1973. 'Nomads from affluence: Notes on the phenomenon of drifter-tourism'. *International Journal of Comparative Sociology*. Vol. 14 (1–2): 89–103.

Cohen, E. 2003. 'Backpacking: Diversity and change'. *Tourism and Cultural Change*. Vol. 1 (2): 95–110.

Coles, A. and Walsh, K. 2010. 'From 'Trucial State' to 'Postcolonial City? The imaginative geographies of British expatriates in Dubai'. *Journal of Ethnic and Migration Studies*. Vol. 36 (8): 1317–1333.

Conradson, D. and Latham, A. 2005a. 'Transnational urbanism: Attending to everyday practices and mobilities'. *Journal of Ethnic and Migration Studies*. Vol. 31 (2): 227–233.

Conradson, D. and A. Latham. 2005b. 'Friendship, networks and transnationality in a world city: Antipodean transmigrants in London'. *Journal of Ethnic and Migration Studies*. Vol. 31 (2): 287–305.

Cresswell, T. 2004. *Place: A Short Introduction*. Oxford: Blackwell.

Cronon, W. 1992. 'Kennecott journey: The paths out of town'. In Cronon, W., Miles, G. and Gitlen, J. (eds) *Under an Open Sky*. New York: Norton.

Delanty, G. 2006. 'The cosmopolitan imagination: Critical cosmopolitanism and social theory'. *The British Journal of Sociology*. Vol. 57 (1): 25–47.

Derrida, J. 1976. *Of Grammatology*. Trans. G.C. Spivak. Baltimore: Johns Hopkins University Press.

Derrida, J. 1978. *Writing and Difference*. Trans. A. Bass. London: Routledge.

Durkheim, E. [1898] 1973. 'Individualism and the intellectuals'. In Bellah, R. (ed.) *On Morality and Society: Selected Writings*. Chicago: University of Chicago Press.

Elias, N. 1965. *The Established and the Outsiders. A Sociological Enquiry into Community Problems*. London: Frank Cass.

Elliott, A. and Lemert, C. 2006. *The New Individualism: The Emotional Costs of Globalisation*. London: Routledge.

Elsrud, T. 1998. 'Time creation in travelling: The taking and making of time among women backpackers'. *Time and Society*. Vol. 7 (2): 309–334.

Farrer, J. 2010. 'New Shanghailanders' or 'New Shanghainese': Western expatriates' narratives of emplacement in Shanghai'. *Journal of Ethnic and Migration Studies*. Vol. 36 (8): 1211–1228.

Farrer, J. 2011. 'Global nightscapes in Shanghai as ethnosexual contact zones'. *Journal of Ethnic and Migration Studies*. Vol. 37 (5): 747–764.

Fechter, A. 2005. 'The other stares back: Experiencing whiteness in Jakarta'. *Ethnography*. Vol. 6 (1): 87–103.

Fechter, A. 2007. *Transnational Lives: Expatriates in Indonesia*. Ashgate: Aldershot.

Fechter, A. 2010. 'Gender, empire, global capitalism: Colonial and corporate expatriate wives'. *Journal of Ethnic and Migration Studies*. Vol. 36 (8): 1279–1297.

Fechter, A. and Hindman, H. (eds) 2011. *Inside the Everyday Lives of Development Workers: The Challenges and Futures of Aidland*. Sterling, VA: Kumarian Press.

Fechter, A. and Walsh, K. 2010. 'Examining 'expatriate' continuities: Postcolonial approaches to mobile professionals'. *Journal of Ethnic and Migration Studies*. Vol. 36 (8): 1197–1210.

Findlay, A., Li, F., Jowett, A. and Skeldon, R. 1996. 'Skilled international migration and the global city: A study of expatriates in Hong Kong'. *Transactions of the Institute of British Geographers*. Vol. 23 (1): 49–61.

Foucault, M. [1976] 1988. *The History of Sexuality, Vol. 1*. London: Penguin.

Foucault, M. 1975. *Discipline and Punish: The Birth of the Prison*. London: Penguin.

Giddens, A. 1991. *Modernity and Self Identity: Self and Society in the Late Modern Age*. Cambridge: Polity Press.

Gluckman, M. 1963. 'Gossip and scandal'. *Current Anthropology*. Vol. 4 (3): 307–316.

Graziosi, B. and Greenwood, E. (eds) 2007. *Homer in the Twentieth Century: Between World Literature and the Western Canon*. Oxford: Oxford University Press.

Hannerz, U. 1996. *Transnational Connections*. London: Routledge.

Hardill, I. 1998. 'Gender perspectives on British expatriate work'. *Geoforum*. Vol. 29 (3): 257–268.

Hatfield, M. 2010. 'Children moving "home"?: Everyday experiences of return migration in highly skilled households'. *Childhood*. Vol. 17 (2): 243–257.

Hetherington, K. 1997. *The Badlands of Modernity: Heterotopia and Social Ordering*. London: Routledge.

Hindman, H. 2008. 'Shopping for a hypernational home: How expatriate women in Kathmandu labour to assuage fear'. In Coles, A. and Fechter, A. (eds) *Gender and Family Among Transnational Professionals*. Routledge: New York.

Hoey, B. (2005). From Pi to Pie: Moral narratives of noneconomic migration and starting over in the postindustrial Midwest. *Journal of Contemporary Ethnography*. Vol. 34 (5): 586–624.

Hugo, G. 2006. 'Expatriates'. In Beilharz, P. and Hogan, T. (eds), *Sociology: Place, Time and Division*, pp. 357–361. Oxford: Oxford University Press.

Hugo, G., Rudd, D. and Harris, K. 2003. *Australia's Diaspora: Its Size, Nature and Policy Implications*. Information Paper No. 80. Canberra: Committee for Economic Development of Australia.

Hunter, S., Swan, E. and Grimes, D. 2010. 'Introduction: Reproducing and resisting whiteness in organizations, policies and places'. *Social Politics*. Vol. 17 (4): 407–422.

Hydrogen Report. 2012. *Global professionals on the move – 2012*. Hydrogen and ESCP Europe. Accessed online at: http://www.hydrogengroup.com/servlet/servlet.FileDownload?file=00PD000000By2ncMAB. Viewed 1 May 2013.

Iyer, P. 2001. *The Global Soul: Jet-Lag, Shopping Malls and the Search for Home*. New York: Random House.

Jackson, P. 1998. 'Constructions of 'whiteness' in the geographical imagination'. *Area*. Vol. 30 (2): 99–106.

Jaeger, C. 1994. *Taming the Dragon*. Chamin de la Sallaz: Gordon and Breach.

Jameson, F. 1988. *The Ideologies of Theory: Essays 1971–1986*. London: Routledge.

Khaleeli, H., Smith, H. and Smith, D. 2013. The great escape: European migrants fleeing the recession. *The Guardian*. Wednesday 30 January 2013. Accessed online at: http://www.guardian.co.uk/global-development/2013/jan/30/great-escape-european-migrants-fleeing-recession. Viewed 30 January 2013.

Kim, N. 2006. ' "Patriarchy is so third world": Korean immigrant women and "migrating" white Western masculinity'. *Social Problems*. Vol. 53 (4): 519–36.

Knapman, C. 1986. *White Women in Fiji 1835–1930: The Ruin of Empire?* Sydney: Allen and Unwin.

Knowles, C. 2005. 'Making whiteness: British lifestyle migrants in Hong Kong'. In Alexander, C. and Knowles, C. (eds) *Making Race Matter: Bodies, Space and Identity*, pp. 90–110. Basingstoke: Palgrave Macmillan.

Kofman, E. 2000. 'The invisibility of skilled female migrants and gender relations in studies of skilled migration in Europe'. *International Journal of Population Geography*. Vol. 6 (1): 45–59.

Kong, L. 1999. 'Globalisation and Singaporean transmigration: Re-imagining and negotiating national identity'. *Political Geography*. Vol. 18 (5): 563–589.

Korpela, M. 2010. 'A Postcolonial imagination? Westerners searching for authenticity in India'. *Journal of Ethnic and Migration Studies*. Vol. 36 (8): 1299–1315.

Koser, K. 2009. *The Global Financial Crisis and International Migration: Policy Implications for Australia*. Sydney: Lowy Institute for International Policy.

Leggett, W. 2005. 'Terror and the colonial imagination at work in the transnational corporate spaces of Jakarta, Indonesia'. *Identities: Global Studies in Culture and Power*. Vol. 12 (2): 271–302.

Leggett, W. 2010. 'Institutionalising the colonial imagination: Chinese middlemen and the transnational corporate office in Jakarta, Indonesia'. *Journal of Ethnic and Migration Studies*. Vol. 36 (8): 1265–1278.

Leonard, P. 2008. 'Migrating identities: Gender, whiteness and Britishness in postcolonial Hong Kong'. *Gender, Place and Culture*. Vol. 15 (1): 45–60.

Leonard, P. 2010a. 'Old colonial or New Cosmopolitan? Changing White identities in the Hong Kong police'. *Social Politics*. Vol. 17 (4): 507–535.

Leonard, P. 2010b. 'Work, identity and change? Post/colonial encounters in Hong Kong'. *Journal of Ethnic and Migration Studies*. Vol. 36 (8): 1247–1263.

Levine, P. (ed.) 2004. *Gender and Empire*. Oxford: Oxford University Press.

Ling, L. 2007. 'Said's exile: Strategic insights for postcolonial feminists'. *Millenium: Journal of International Studies*. Vol. 36 (1): 135–146.

MacCannell, D. [1979] 1999. *The Tourist: A New Theory of the Leisure Class*. Berkeley: University of California Press.

MacGregor, J. 2005. *One Billion Customers: Lessons from the Front Lines of Doing Business in China*. New York: Free Press.

MacKenzie-Grieve, A. 1952. *A Race of Green Ginger*. London: Putnam.

Mahler, S. and Pessar, P. 2006. 'Gender matters: Ethnographers bring gender from the periphery towards the core of migration studies'. *International Migration Review*. Vol. 40 (1): 27–63.

Malpas, J. 1999. *Place and Experience: A Philosophical Topography*. Cambridge: Cambridge University Press.

Manderson, L. and Jolly, M. (eds) (1997). *Sites of Desire, Economies of Pleasure: Sexualities in Asia and the Pacific*. Chicago: University of Chicago Press.

Massey, D. 2005. *For Space*. London: Sage.

McNay, L. 1999. 'Gender, habitus and the field: Pierre Bourdieu and the limits of reflexivity'. *Theory, Culture and Society*. Vol. 16 (1): 95–117.

Merton, R. [1938] 1973. *The Sociology of Science: Theoretical and Empirical Investigations*. Chicago: University of Chicago Press.

Murray, R., Harding, D., Angus, T., Gillespie, R. and Arora, H. 2012. *Emigration from the UK*. Second Edition. Research Report 68. November. Home Office: London.

Nowicka, M. 2007. 'Mobile locations: Construction of home in a group of mobile transnational professionals'. *Global Networks*. Vol. 7 (1): 69–86.

Nye, J. 2010. 'American and Chinese power after the financial crisis'. *The Washington Quarterly*. Vol. 33 (4): 269–285.

Oliver, C. 2007. 'Imagined communitas: Older migrants and aspirational mobility'. In Amit, V. (ed.) *Going First Class? New Approaches to Privileged Travel and Movement*. Berghahn: Oxford.

Oliver, C. 2008. *Retirement Migration: Paradoxes of Ageing.* London: Routledge.

Ong, A. 1999. *Flexible Citizenship: The Cultural Logics of Transnationality.* Durham, NC: Duke University Press.

Organization for Economic Cooperation and Development. 2002. *The International Mobility of the Highly Skilled.* Paris: OECD.

O'Reilly, C. 2006. 'From drifter to gap-year tourist: Mainstreaming backpacker travel'. *Annals of Tourism Research*, 33(4), 998–1017.

Organization for Economic Cooperation and Development. 2003. *Trends in International Migration.* Paris: OECD.

Organization for Economic Cooperation and Development. 2004. *A New Database on the International Mobility of the Highly Skilled and Policy Options.* Paris: OECD.

Papademetriou, D., Sumption, M. and Terrazas, A. 2010. *Migration and Immigrants Two Years after the Financial Collapse: Where Do We Stand?* Washington: Migration Policy Institute.

Park, R. [1928] 1969. Human migration and the marginal man. In Sennett, R. (ed.) *The Classic Essays on the Culture of Cities.* New York: Appleton-Century-Crofts.

Parsons, T. 1966. *Societies: Evolutionary and Comparative Perspectives.* Englewood Cliffs, NJ: Prentice-Hall.

Patty, A. 2011. Drained HSC students take gap to recharge. *Sydney Morning Herald.* Accessed online at: http://www.smh.com.au/national/education/ drained-hsc-students-take-gap-to-recharge-20110107-19itk.html. Viewed 21 October 2011.

Perkowski, J. 2008. *Managing the Dragon: How I'm Building a Billion-Dollar Business in China.* New York: Random House.

Pew Research Center. 2013. Pervasive gloom about the world economy. Accessed online at: http://www.pewglobal.org/2012/07/12/pervasive-gloom-about-the-world-economy/. Viewed 21 March 2013.

Pierson, R. 1998. 'Introduction'. In Pierson, R. and Chaudhuri, N. (eds) *Nation, Empire and Colony: Historicizing Race and Gender.* Indianapolis: Indiana University Press.

Plomin, J. 2001. 'Gap year popularity soars'. *The Guardian.* 13 September. Accessed online at: http://www.guardian.co.uk/education/2001/sep/13/ highereducation.uk. Viewed 5 December 2009.

Portes, A. 2010. 'Migration and social change: Some conceptual reflections'. *Journal of Ethnic and Migration Studies.* Vol. 36 (10): 1537–1563.

Powell, B. 2004. *Homer.* Malden, MA: Blackwell.

Powell, J. 2006. *Jacques Derrida: A Biography.* London: Continuum.

Prasso, S. 2005. *Asian Mystique: Dragon Ladies, Geisha Girls, and Our Fantasies of the Exotic Orient.* New York: Public Affairs.

Raban, J. 1974. *Soft City.* Glasgow: Hamish Hamilton.

Rifkin, J. 2000. *The End of Work: The Decline of the Global Work-Force and the Dawn of the Post-Market Era*, 2nd edn. London: Penguin.

Robinson, M. and Phipps, A. 2003. 'Worlds passing by: Journeys of culture and cultural journeys'. *Tourism and Cultural Change.* Vol. 1 (1): 1–10.

Robinson, W. 2004. *A Theory of Global Capitalism: Production, Class and State in a Transnational World.* Baltimore, MD: The John Hopkins University Press.

Rosenthal, E. 2005. *The Era of Choice: The Ability to Choose and Its Transformation of Contemporary Life.* Cambridge, MA: MIT Press.

Ross, T. 2012. 'UK taxes are driving middle-class brain drain'. *The Telegraph*, 14–20 November, p. 10.

Rostow, W. [1960] 1990. *Stages of Economic Growth: A Non-Communist Manifesto*, 3rd edn. Cambridge: Cambridge University Press.

Rundell, J. 2004. 'Strangers, citizens and outsiders: Otherness, multiculturalism and the cosmopolitan imaginary in mobile societies'. *Thesis Eleven*. Vol. 78 (1): 85–101.

Said, E. 1978. *Orientalism*. New York: Pantheon.

Said, E. 2001. *Reflections on Exile and Other Essays*. Cambridge, MA: Harvard University Press.

Sassen, S. 2001. *The Global City: London, New York, Tokyo*. Princeton: Princeton University Press.

Scheff, T. 1994. *Microsociology: Discourse, Emotion and Social Structure*. Chicago: University of Chicago Press.

Scheffler, S. 1999. 'Conceptions of cosmopolitanism'. *Utalitas*. Vol. 11(3): 256–276.

Schultz, T. 1963. *The Economic Value of Education*. New York: Columbia University Press.

Schutz, A. 1944. 'The stranger: An essay in social psychology'. *American Journal of Sociology*. Vol. 49 (6): 499–507.

Scott, J. 1999. *Gender and the Politics of History*. New York: Colombia University Press.

Seligson, H. 2009. 'American graduates finding jobs in China'. *The New York Times*, 11 August. Accessed online at: www.nytimes.com/2009/08/11/business/economy/11expats.-html. Viewed 7 September 2009.

Selmer, J. 2004. 'Expatriates' hesitation and the localization of Western business operations in China'. *The International Journal of Human Resource Management*. Vol. 15 (6): 1094–1107.

Sennett, R. 1998. *The Corrosion of Character*. New York: Norton.

Sennett, R. 2006. *The Culture of the New Capitalism*. London: Yale University Press.

Simmel, G. [1900] 1978. 'The Stranger'. In Wolff, K. (ed.) *The Sociology of Georg Simmel*. London: The Free Press.

Simmel, G. [1907] 1978. 'The metropolis and mental life'. In Wolff, K. (ed.) *The Sociology of Georg Simmel*. London: The Free Press.

Skeldon, R. 2010. *The Current Global Economic Crisis and Migration: Policies and Practice in Origin and Destination*. University of Sussex and DFID. Working Paper T-32.

Sklair, L. 2001. *The Transnational Capitalist Class*. Oxford: Blackwell.

Smith, M. 2001. *Transnational Urbanism: Locating Globalisation*. Oxford: Blackwell.

Soja, E. 1989. *Postmodern Geographies: The Reassertion of Space in Critical Social Theory*. London: Verso Press.

Steegmuller, F. 1996. *Flaubert in Egypt: A Sensibility on Tour*. London: Penguin.

Steger, M. 2002. *Globalism: The New Market Ideology*. Lanham, MD: Rowman and Littlefield.

Stein, M. 1960. *The Eclipse of Community*. Princeton: Princeton University Press.

Svaek, M. 2010. 'On the move: Emotions and human mobility'. *Journal of Ethnic and Migration Studies*. Vol. 36 (1): 865–880.

Svasek, M. and Skrbis, Z. 2007. 'Passions and powers: Emotions and globalisation'. *Identities: Global Studies in Culture and Power*. Vol. 14 (4): 367–371.

Taylor, C. 1985. *Human Agency and Language*. Cambridge: Cambridge University Press.

Trundle, C. 2009. 'Romance tourists, foreign wives or retirement migrants? Cross-cultural marriage in Florence, Italy'. In Benson, M. and O'Reilly, K. (eds) *Lifestyle Migration: Expectations, Aspirations and Experiences*. Farnham: Ashgate.

Turner, B. 1994. 'Postmodern culture/modern citizens'. In van Steenbergen, B. (ed.) *The Condition of Citizenship*. London: Sage.

Turner, B. 2000. 'Cosmopolitan virtue: Loyalty and the city'. In Insin, E. (ed.) *Democracy, Citizenship and the Global City*. London: Routledge.

Turner, B. and Rojek, C. 2001. *Society and Culture: Principles of Scarcity and Solidarity*. London: Sage.

Turner, V. 1969. *The Ritual Process: Structure and Anti-Structure*. Chicago: Aldine Publishing.

Twine, G. and Gallagher, C. 2008. 'The future of whiteness: A map of the 'third wave'. *Journal of Ethnic and Racial Studies*. Vol. 31 (1): 4–24.

Urry, J. 2000. *Sociology Beyond Societies: Mobilities for the Twenty-First Century*. London: Routledge.

Van den Abbeele, G. 1980. 'Sightseers: The tourist as theorist'. *Diacritics*. Vol. 10 (4): 2–14.

Walsh, K. 2006. ' "Dad says I'm tied to a shooting star!" Grounding (research on) British expatriate belonging'. *Area*. Vol. 38 (3): 268–278.

Walsh, K. 2007. ' "It got very debauched, very Dubai!" Heterosexual intimacy amongst single British expatriates'. *Social and Cultural Geography*. Vol. 8 (4): 507–533.

Walsh, K. 2012. 'Emotion and migration: British transnationals in Dubai'. *Environment and Planning D: Society and Space*. Vol. 30 (1): 43–59.

Walsh, K., Shen, H. and Willis, K. 2008. 'Heterosexuality and migration in Asia'. *Gender, Place and Culture*. Vol. 15 (6): 575–595.

Warner, M. 2002. 'Publics and counterpublics'. *Public Culture*. Vol. 14 (1): 49–90.

Weber, M. [1905] 2001. 'The protestant ethic and the spirit of capitalism'. London: Routledge.

Williams, A. and Hall, C. 2002. 'Tourism, migration, circulation and mobility: The contingencies of time and place'. In Williams, A. and Hall, C. (eds) *Tourism and Migration: New Relationships Between Production and Consumption*. London: Kluwer Academic Publishers.

Williams, R. 1997. 'South Asian religions in the United States'. In Hinnells, J. (ed.) *A New Handbook of Living Religions*. London: Penguin.

Willis, K. and Yeoh, B. (2002). 'Gendering transnational communities: A comparison of Singaporean and British migrants in China'. *Geoforum*. Vol. 33 (4): 553–565.

Wood, F. 1998. *No Dogs and Not Many Chinese: Treaty Port Life in China 1843–1943*. London: John Murray Publishers.

Xiamen Municipal Government. 2006. *Population*. Accessed online at: http://english.xm.-gov.cn/xiamenoverview/population/200808/t20080827_274166.html. Viewed 23 April 2009.

Yeoh, B. 2004. 'Global/globalizing cities'. *Progress in Human Geography*. Vol. 23 (4): 607–616.

Yeoh, B. and Huang, S. 2011. 'Introduction: Fluidity and friction in talent migration. *Journal of Ethnic and Migration Studies*. Vol. 37 (5): 681–690.

Yeoh, B. and Willis, K. 2005. 'Singaporean and British transmigrants in China and the cultural politics of "contact zones"'. *Journal of Ethnic and Migration Studies*. Vol. 31 (2): 269–285.

Yoshihara, M. 2003. *Embracing the East: White women and American Orientalism*. Oxford: Oxford University Press.

Zukin, S. 1991. *Landscapes of Power: From Detroit to Disneyworld*. Berkeley: University of California Press.

Index